Allen Griffin challenges us [barcode] tianity in *Undefeated*. It is i without feeling convicted to li̲̅ ̲̅ ̲̅ ̲̅ ̲̅ ̲̅ ̲̅adically! You will be reminded that we are called to win the battle against the enemy and will learn how to prepare for that battle. While reading this book, you will hear the voice of God yelling, "You can and you will defeat every enemy!" A must-read.

—*Jeff Hillier*
Lead pastor, CPC Ottawa

I have found a kindred spirit in Allen Griffin, especially in his "ADHD version" of Scripture and vivid life stories that remind us of the power of our testimony. Allen drives home the scripture that "you shall win them by the word of your testimony" in a way that only Allen can. This book can rekindle a pastor, motivate a parent, and truly inspire young people to know that they are a mighty army and are able to take the fight to the giants in their lives.

—*Charles Boyd*
National Youth Director, IPHC

Allen Griffin has penned a book of such magnitude it will be a catalyst for exploding your faith. Don't miss reading one page of this book! You'll discover how to recognize your God-designed directive in life and lay hold of it with a passionate force.

—*Dr. Kent Ingle*
President, Southeastern University

Undefeated is a must-read for leaders who want to *first* lead themselves. If your confession is "I am, I can. I will be all God designed me to be," *Undefeated* is a must-read!

—*Sam Farina*
Evangelist

Allen's passion for God and excellence in communication comes through in this exciting and challenging book. His unique presentation of the timeless truths of God's Word will leave readers laughing, but then slammed with the conviction that God is calling us to live life undefeated.

—*EUGENE SMITH*
Lead pastor, City Church Orlando

Allen Griffin's book *Undefeated* is an outstanding work that challenges the mind and strengthens the heart. His book uses Scripture and men and women of the Bible to inspire you to live out the words of the Bible, accomplish more, and understand what it really means to love God with all your heart, soul, mind, and strength. I encourage everyone to take the time and read this book. It is a real life changer.

—*RANDAL ROSS*
Senior pastor, Calvary Church

Thought provoking, instructive, engaging…*Undefeated* will stir your emotions with practical biblical truths and multigenerational allure. Al Griffin rouses us to testify, witness, and "pick a fight with hell" for the advancement of God's kingdom.

—*DR. RAY BERRYHILL*
Senior pastor, Evangel World Outreach Center

Rev. Allen Griffin has a knack for discovering humor and insight that promote a fruitful life for God's kingdom. There is much wisdom to gain and truth to glean as you read this book. I recommend this book and other writings

Rev. Griffin has contributed for the enrichment of believers from all backgrounds and fellowships as well as my own.

—*DR. GEORGE O. WOOD*
General superintendent, Assemblies of God

Undefeated is a wild ride through the provocative testaments of heroes, both biblical and modern. Allen Griffin enfaces hilarity and thoughtful biblical revelation to help the reader grasp the deeper understandings of a powerful and influential Christian life. You will laugh and learn through this book, and I heartily recommended it as a shot of spiritual caffeine to all!

—*SCOTT WILSON*
Senior pastor, The Oaks Fellowship in Red Oak, Texas
Author of Act Normal

Allen Griffin is the definition of a champion—the Michael Jordan of evangelism! Taking his words to a whole new level, Allen pens an incredible, powerful book. His writing is just like his speaking—contagious, relevant, uplifting, and inspiring. *Undefeated* is a book you won't be able to put down—a high-flyin', death-defyin', 360 slam dunk!

—*TRAVIS HEARN*
Team chaplain, Phoenix Suns
Senior pastor, Impact Church

It is a joy to commend the book *Undefeated* by Allen Griffin. This manuscript is more than a "battle cry" for Christians and their leaders; it is a "battle plan" for victory and success! The spiritual insights and ministry on these pages will be valuable to every true believer who is waging warfare against our enemy. Evangelist Griffin presents clear and effective instructions and inspiration that will lead warriors of Calvary from the jeopardy of battle to the ranks of the undefeated! Read it to be blessed, encouraged, equipped, and victorious for our Lord!

—REV. TERRY RABURN
District superintendent, Peninsular Florida
District Council, Assemblies of God

Allen does a phenomenal job of putting you in the middle of one of the most famous stories in the Bible, the slaying of Goliath by David. Then he weaves this story into a manual for Christians to train, serve, and become victorious soldiers for Jesus Christ. Practical, easy to read, and full of piercing truth!

—STU JOHNSON
USAF colonel (retired)
Executive administrator, Grace International
Churches and Ministries, Inc.

Allen Griffin has issued a clarion call for a generation to awaken to the greatness that lies within them. With incredible clarity and pinpoint accuracy he challenges the believer to rise up in the power of God and engage the forces of evil. When you do, you will discover that God never has and never will be overwhelmed. As you read this book, you will awaken to this mighty revelation; your destiny is to be...UNDEFEATED!

—JIM RALEY
Senior pastor, Calvary Christian Center,
Ormond Beach, Florida, and author of Hell's Spells

Allen Griffin never ceases to amaze me. His new book, *Undefeated*, has taken his extraordinary communication skill from the stage to the page. Allen moves you into action as you read this truly inspiring book. I highly recommend it to anyone needing an encouraging word. Well done, my friend.

—RICK ROSS
Lead pastor, Concord First Assembly of God

Be prepared to be motivated! *Undefeated* will deepen a desire to step out and fulfill God's calling with greater urgency in your life.

—REV. MARVIN B. BEGAY
Senior pastor, Canyon Day Assembly of God
Youth director, Native American Fellowship
of the Assemblies of God

What if you had a coach to remind you that your destiny is not erased, inspire you to rise up and challenge the giants in your life, and provoke you to live up to the level of your potential? In *Undefeated* Allen Griffin takes the form of an Ephesians 4:11 coach called evangelist and challenges readers to live up to their God-birthed, sin-conquering, soul-winning identity that Jesus Christ says His followers would exhibit. What are you waiting for? Let the coach blow his whistle and summon the greatness that is within. You'll never be the same again!

—NATE RUCH
Senior pastor, Emmanuel Christian Center
Former vice president of university relations
and enrollment, North Central University

UNDEFEATED

ALLEN GRIFFIN

CHARISMA
HOUSE

Cover design by Lisa Rae Cox

Visit the author's website at www.agministries.com.

Library of Congress Control Number: 2013902999
International Standard Book Number: 978-1-62136-026-1
E-book ISBN: 978-1-62136-027-8

20 21 22 23 24 — 8 7 6 5 4
Printed in the United States of America

This book is dedicated in loving memory of my father, Herbert Lee Griffin Sr. Without my father's humor and wisdom my life would have been filled with meaningless chatter. My dad was more than a provider and leader throughout my life. Dad was my Gibraltar. Thank you for teaching me how to work hard and to never leave anything important undone or unspoken. I love you, Daddy!

CONTENTS

ACKNOWLEDGMENTS

Rev. M. Wayne and Kathy Benson
Rev. Jim and Dawn Raley and family
Rev. Randy and Jelly Valimont and family
Rev. Dave and Brenda Roever
Rev. Reggie and Michele Dabbs and Dominic
Rev. George Wood
Allen Griffin Ministries staff
Calvary Christian Center family and staff
Rev. Sam Farina
Rev. Scotty Gibbons
Rev. Jeff and Jane Grenell and family
Rev. Nathan and Jodi Ruch
Rev. Mark and Michelle Benson and family
Larry Farmer and family
Rev. Rick Ross and family
Ofc. Dave Gillem
Torrence and Bethany Jackson and beautiful "jits"
Matt and Jamie Roever and family
Mark and Jamie Kenney and family
Rev. Randal Ross and family
Rev. Galen and Davis
Rev. Pat Shatzline
Angel and Darlene Watson and family
Rev. Al and Jinny Force and family

The Katinas and family
John and Nancy Bitow and family
Trent and Keisha Cory and kiddos
Rev. Lee and Sandy McFarland and family
Rev. Patrick "Packy" and Janet Thompson and family
Rev. Roger and Lisa Coles and cute baby
that I am going to steal someday!
J. Jason and Corey Toro and family
Rev. Shawn and Sonny Hennessy and family
Adelbert LeeYee
Rev. Aaron Penton
Rev. Ray Allen Berryhill
Rev. Rich and Robyn Wilkerson
Rev. Rich Jr. and DawnCheré Wilkerson
Taylor Wilkerson
Graham Wilkerson
Jonfulton Wilkerson and family

And special words to my wonderful family without
whom I couldn't imagine a life worth living:
Florence Miriam Griffin: Mom, you are my JOY!
George and Dagma Daniel
Sascha and Shevanthi Rabkin
Joe and Roshini Houser
Jimmy Griffin
Johnny Griffin
Rev. Herbert Lee Griffin Jr. and family
Kevin and Anthea Green
And to my precious ones, I love you forever!

Hashmareen Griffin, you are the heart
of everything I am and do.
Israel and Isaiah Griffin, I'm so proud of you!
You boys are why I strive to be a better man.

To my Lord and Savior Jesus Christ: Thank
You for letting me be on Your team!

PART 1

THE PROBLEM:
UNDEFEATED SIN

HE CHEERING WAS SO RAUCOUS THE YOUNG hero's ears were ringing and a wave of emotion overtook him. People from all over the city—soldiers, tentmakers, blacksmiths, and messengers—ran to keep up with the victory procession. It seemed that everyone wanted to see him enter Jerusalem, and they would clamber through a din of revelers to catch a glimpse. "All this is for me?" He paused and quickly wiped sweat and tears from his eyes. He never imagined the people's response would be so intense.

In his right hand was a trophy like no other: dripping with blood and spittle, covered in sackcloth, riddled with flies, was the head of Goliath from Gath. This powerful man had stood his ground against Israel for more than a month in battle array. Yet it was no famous soldier who had dispatched this nine-foot-tall enemy. It was a part-time soldier/sheepherder named

David! The victory celebration rose to a fever pitch as songs broke out all over Jerusalem: *Saul has killed his thousands in battle and David his tens of thousands!*

As if by some form of intuition the ornate doors of the palace courtyard opened, and the reveling procession paused at the presence of the royal guard of the king. Crimson flags and crests snapped and popped, as they flapped back and forth in the gentle northwest breeze. King Saul motioned with one hand, and the musicians and dancers immediately ceased their performance. The air seemed to still on command and an eagle's cry rang out overhead in the silence while the king looked intently at the young conqueror. The king's powerful voice broke the anxious tension and boomed over the courtyard with a plying question: "Whose son are you, young man?" David answered, "I am the son of your servant Jesse the Bethlehemite" (1 Sam. 17:58).

All of a sudden rock-and-roll music started with a face-melting guitar solo and fireworks sprayed a crimson flower of fire across the sky! The people started singing in four-part harmony "We Are the Champions"...and double cheeseburgers were handed out to every man, woman, boy, and girl....Fried chicken trees bloomed, and cotton candy bushes gave of their fruit, green diamonds, purple horseshoes, and rivers of Kool-Aid.... Then a unicorn showed up and...

OK, OK, that last paragraph never happened. (It *is* a fantasy of mine!) But David still *did* kill Goliath.

Just like you, I am tired of the telling and retelling of stories from a historic perspective without a shred of creativity or insight. I have heard the sermons about this story, and many of them are snooze-fests; I wouldn't put you through that. I grew up in church, and so many times I would hear the obvious so much that I soon became oblivious to it all. Instead I want to know: What's my takeaway from this story? What else happened? What was going on here? Why was Goliath so stinking big? What does this have to do with me? There's much we can learn from the battle in 1042 BC when Israel faced off with the Philistines in an epic battle that almost wasn't—if we pay attention.

Saul was God's first king over the people of Israel. They had cried and complained for so long that they wanted a great leader like all the other nations that were surrounding them. God finally gave in to their earnest desires with a strict warning of obedience to His ultimate rule and the king as His authority. It was only two years before direct disobedience reared its ugly head in the leadership of Saul, and he was immediately rejected by the Lord as the king of Israel. Now we find King Saul in a stagnant leadership position: tormented by evil spirits sent by the Lord and unable to rise above his own selfish ambition to become the leader God wanted him to be.

There is something you need to know. God has a specific directive for you. He wants you to accomplish more, be more, do more...but a one-ton problem stands in your way. Don't be lackadaisical and just simply wait for something to happen to you. There is an obstacle that wants to rob you of your destiny, and it is big and small, here and there, every day…Let's discover and dispatch this foe together and *"kill the champion!"*

CHAPTER 1

YOUR VALLEY OF ELAH

F IRST SAMUEL 17 DESCRIBES THE LOCATION and the setup of a classic biblical battle between the Israelites and the Philistines in Ephes Dammim. The Israelites stood on the mountain on one side and the Philistines on the mountain on the other side, with the valley of Elah between them. The size of the two armies must be quite vast as the Bible describes the camps of both forces as stretching two and a half to three miles long between Socoh and Azekah. (I always thought that Azekah would be a good name for a daughter, but my wife said no.)

I don't know about you, but I always seem to read the Bible imagining that I am there and wondering what I would do if I faced the same or similar circumstances. I actually see myself as a warrior in these battles, and I try to put myself in the shoes (or the sandals!) of these particular heroes. I want to know what makes them tick and why, and how they did many of the amazing (and foolish) things that they did. While I read this story, I feel like I am David, and this is my chance to prove myself and show the world my skills! Yeah, I'm the man…

Enter Goliath! A nine-foot-nine-inch-tall beast of a man stands before the ranks of Israel and challenges them to send one man down to the valley to fight for the fate of the nations. This man's armor weighed 220 pounds, and his spear's head alone weighed 15 pounds. This man's armor weighed more than the average man's *body*. Can you imagine a man who stands so tall that the top of his head would be in the middle of the nets of an NBA basketball hoop? He would be able to touch the top of the backboard of the basketball hoop without leaving his feet. Goliath would have weighed more than 400 pounds. His shoe size would be a 32. (I can imagine neighborhood cows running for their lives when he broke a sandal walking the hillsides of his hometown. The amount of leather it could take to make one of his shoes should have been terrifying to them! Yikes!) To imagine that the tallest player in the National Basketball Association was Yao Ming at *only* seven foot six puts Goliath in rarified air. Goliath would dwarf Shaquille Rashaun O'Neal (whose name means "little warrior"[1]) by at least two and a half feet. This champion from Gath was so big that his armor was like having a large professional athlete duct-taped to his chest as a bulletproof vest! I don't think anyone would mess with this guy. Get the point? This dude was *big*!

Every day in the morning and in the evening Goliath would come forward and present himself to the Israelite army. He would call the army out and shame them and their God with cunning derogatory and inflammatory curses. This continued for forty days before our hero showed up on the scene. What is quite astonishing for a battlefield showdown is that the Israelite army refused to fight Goliath and the Philistines the whole time! What were they waiting for? Why would they not strike out at this enemy? Wasn't this battle a guaranteed win? God had instructed Saul to evict the enemy out of the Promised Land of Israel—the same land that Joshua the son of Nun had been fighting for, removing all the occupants before he died of old age. It was now Saul's turn, but it seemed he was faltering in his divine moment. All he had to do was give the order, and the Lord would be with them in battle and the enemy would be destroyed.

King Saul was no slouch with a sword and a spear. Having already killed thousands of enemy troops, this first king of Israel was a mighty warrior. First Samuel 9 describes Saul as a "choice and handsome son" and tells us that he was head and shoulders taller than any of the people (v. 2). Saul would have been over seven feet tall, and he weighed in at a svelte 300 pounds. Don't you wish that the Bible described *you* as the most handsome person in the land? When the Word of God says that you are the most handsome... *you must really look great!*

I can understand why King Saul did not want to fight Goliath. I mean, after all, this Goliath guy was a formidable and fear-inducing opponent. Did you notice the detail distinctly missing from the description of Goliath that I so vividly and eloquently (*ahem!*) placed before you? That's right, I never used the word *giant*. The Bible itself doesn't describe Goliath as a giant; the Bible describes him as a "champion." This was a new revelation to me as I have heard and have described this huge behemoth as a "giant" for much of my life. It's even become a cultural icon; we refer to this story as "David versus the Giant," or we say we ourselves are "facing the giants." All of this refers to the physical stature of this opponent, but let's stick to the *truth* of the Bible's statements about Goliath.

Who Is Your Champion?

So, Goliath was a "champion"—but what does that mean? We know that in sports and in life a champion is usually someone who wins. It could easily be said that a champion doesn't lose or that a champion never loses. (Kind of like the 1972 Miami Dolphins football team...I'm just sayin'.) Goliath was the Philistines' mightiest warrior, and he was willing to bet his undefeated record in battle against the very best that Israel had to offer.

But wait! There *is* a champion in your life right now. Who is your champion? Right away many followers of Christ would shout from the rooftops that Jesus Christ is their champion, never truly contemplating their situation. Much like the Israelite army, we wake up every day and put on the armor of God: the helmet of salvation, the breastplate of righteousness, the shield of faith, the sword of the Spirit, which is the Word of God, the belt of truth, shod our feet with the preparation of the gospel of peace, and yet we rarely ever use them! These are all weapons of advancement in our fight to make Jesus famous in our communities.

Have you been using your armor properly? When is the last time you shared your faith with someone? When is the last time you had the honor of leading someone to a divine relationship with Christ? *That* was the last time you fought and won this battle. That was the last time you trusted and lived as the warrior God wants us to be.

What was the purpose of this King Saul anyway? To reign and rule over God's people with power and a righteous hand? That sounds really great and important, but that's not what God called Saul to do. In 1 Samuel 9:16 the Lord spoke to Samuel concerning Saul: "Tomorrow about this time I will send you a man from the land of Benjamin, and you shall anoint him commander over My people Israel, that he may save My people from the hand of the Philistines; for I have looked upon My people, because their cry has come to Me." It is quite clear that God's purpose for the first king of Israel was to fight the enemy and deliver the people from Philistine oppression. Fully possessing the Promised Land meant eradicating the people who lived there through whatever means necessary…in other words, war.

You were made for war. You were created with a divine purpose that may seem a bit odd and strange: *to kill people and take their stuff!* Before you throw this book across the room and declare me a heretic, hear me out. We are to kill sin...kill it in us and in all those around us. The apostle Paul wrote to the church in Galatians 2:20: "I have been crucified with Christ; it is no longer I who live, but Christ lives in me; and the life which I now live in the flesh I live by faith in the Son of God, who loved me and gave Himself for me." Paul takes this understanding to another dimension. We are to first kill sin in us by putting the sinful nature inside of us to death. The next step is to go out and tell others how they can be free and help them kill the sin in their lives, thereby adding their souls to the kingdom of God. We therefore, are killing (sin) and taking (adding) the stuff (people) for the King (the heavenly Father)! Now, I dare you to say this out loud: "My job in God's kingdom is to kill people and take their stuff!" (Make sure you are not saying this on an airplane....I will not vouch for you, nor will I bail you out of prison.)

Can you imagine being one of the thousands of Israelite soldiers who arose, every morning and every night, to put on heavy armor and march? It would take a soldier quite some time to dress with all the chainmail and equipment that was required to prepare himself for battle. Yet after all this preparation and care every morning and evening, still *no one* fought? Not one person even yelled back at Goliath? No one even kicked dirt in his direction? No one threw even one spear? Why?

Goliath was not just the champion of the Philistines; it appears that he was also the champion of the Israelites. He was *un*defeated because he was *un*challenged by the people of God. If the men of Israel would have just tried...if they had lifted their arms...if they would have just arisen and pursued victory, it was all within their reach! But the task seemed ominous to the men of Israel, and they forsook their spiritual training and history, which had proven that Israel was mighty because of their God, not their physical prowess.

During that time it was common for opposing forces to put forward a "champion" fighter who would represent the whole nation in a man-to-man fight to the death. This fight would be presented on the battlefield in full view of both armies. Most times this tribute fight was instituted to avoid massive bloodshed and loss of life. I would guess the results never ended in a satisfactory situation for either party and chaos would still ensue, but the hearts of the defeated army would more than likely be sunk, as their very best warrior would be dead. Morale and spirit are vital to warriors on the field, and such a victory by the champion would propel the victor to triumph and repel the loser to depths of doubt that *would most certainly* end in defeat.

The fear of failure can often motivate action, but the fear of God will cause us to do something even greater, something that has eternal significance.

Israel was stymied in their attempt to possess the land. This huge man stood in their way, and there was no one to face him. What were they going to do? Nothing...that's what most of us do. We all have challenges and obstacles that stand in our way, but very few of us actually grab the opportunity to knock that champion down and cut off its head!

Whose Side Are You On?

Let's not mince words here. We are soldiers, and we are supposed to fight! What is our fight? Our fight is to live an extraordinary life of devotion to our God and make His name great in all our circumstances. When we are winning the battle on the inside, it becomes much easier to share our faith in Jesus Christ with everyone around us.

Let's discover where you stand with a few questions:

1. Is Christ the undefeated force of your life?

2. What is in your life that you wish wasn't there?

3. When was the last time you shared Jesus with unbelievers?

4. Why do we make such light of sharing our faith?

While these questions were being posed to you, maybe you hold doubt about the Lord's demands and commands in this area, thinking they are somehow debatable or unreasonable. I assure you, the Lord feels strongly about His orders. Read here the last thing He said to the disciples in Acts 1:8: "But you shall receive power when the Holy Spirit has come upon you; and you shall be witnesses to Me in Jerusalem, and in all Judea and Samaria, and to the end of the earth." When Jesus rose from the dead, Mark 16:15 recorded Him as saying:

"Go into all the world and preach the gospel to every creature."

Even if we try to obey Jesus's command in Matthew 22:37–40, we must acknowledge that in order to truly love someone, you have to care about their relationship (or lack thereof) with Christ. Here is Jesus's instruction to us:

> Jesus said to him, "'You shall love the LORD your God with all your heart, with all your soul, and with all your mind.' This is the first and great commandment. And the second is like it: 'You shall love your neighbor as yourself.' On these two commandments hang all the Law and the Prophets."

Have you been living this commandment, fighting for the lives of the people around you, or are you simply too busy?

The enemy of your soul wants you to live on the defense and not on the offense. He wants you to continually live a life in which all you do is "try not to sin." But Jesus did not come to live a life of perfection on the earth, get murdered, rise from the dead, and then give you the power of the Holy Spirit so that you could just "try not to sin." The life of complacency is living life on the defense. Casual Christianity will make you a casualty of this war.

We must live lives of offense. Offense means that we are scoring in the game! How do we score? The simple effects of scoring are to add numbers to the account of your team or organization. Scoring spiritually adds to the accounting of precious people saved by God's wonderful grace. Have you added population to eternity for the kingdom of God? Is "Team Heaven" better with your star in the game? When I watch basketball games, the crowd cheers each and every time their favorite team scores. That could be as many as sixty to seventy times in one game! The enemy does not want to make you evil, just irrelevant. Luke 15 declares that all of heaven rejoices when one sinner comes to repentance and faith in Christ (v. 7). That's a score! Imagine how huge the party must be going on in heaven as people are coming to faith in Christ every few seconds. Have you given heaven a reason to rejoice lately? Are the angels dancing because you went to work today and made Jesus known to a coworker who received Him?

Find Yourself in Christ

Undefeated sin will stop us in our tracks. It will keep us from faith-filled development and growth in our relationship with God. Without that divine relationship we are destined to fail. The fruits of this type of living are evident in all that we do. We can lose focus and become so selfish and narcissistic that we do or don't do things based solely on our feelings and the end benefits to ourselves.

I've noticed that when we find ourselves living on the defense and not on the offense, we become stymied in our identity and purpose for living. I watched a documentary once about a world-famous athlete who lost his way and turned to drugs to "find himself." His career melting away in the trials and tribulations from his evident drug use, he still kept traveling around the world to try to find his purpose in life. After years of wasted time and talent, this man finally settled on the thought that his purpose was to be a good father to his children and care for the needs of his family who had loved him through all his misgivings. I often wish I had the ear of these brothers and sisters while they are struggling to "find themselves." You can only find yourself in the one whom you serve. If you serve the Lord, your identity is found in Christ, your Creator. Everything else and anything else is a shadow of truth and more than likely a lie.

These lies about ourselves are easy to believe, but they are usually due to undefeated sin in our lives that we are unwilling to acknowledge. We can become so oblivious, or numb, to this undefeated sin over time that eventually we miss out on the life God has for us—that of a victorious warrior for Him! Let's take a look now at one of the main reasons we become oblivious to sin— fragmented realities. Read on.

CHAPTER 2

FRAGMENTED REALITIES

I HAVE DISCOVERED A TERRIBLE TRUTH IN MY life...I have "multiple personhood disorder"! Far too often I live as if I am several different people. This augmented reality has allowed me to do things that I know aren't right and then park those actions in a corner and never once have to deal with them. You see, these actions don't exist in my present situation. I compartmentalize them. I separate myself into distinct zones of living where I can seamlessly blend into my environment and no one sees me as out of place. My goal has been for people to like me and for me not to make a fool out of myself. While these goals are quite ambitious for one such as myself, I have actually become pretty good at maintaining the status quo. But this has brought me much misery as I have missed so many opportunities to be someone who made a difference and do something for God that matters.

Some time ago I was on a plane from Sydney, Australia, to Chicago, Illinois, and I was exhausted. A mixture of the spanning of multiple time zones and rigorous activities had resulted in a tired body and mind. The last thing I wanted to do at that point was talk to anyone. As I got on the plane and took my seat, I noticed an older woman enter the plane with red eyes and a handkerchief in her hand. Immediately the Lord spoke to me that I needed to share His love with her. "Ugh! God, I am so tired! Seriously? I just finished speaking to thousands of people about You. Isn't that enough?"

I wish that I could tell you that this "professional evangelist" jumped up right then and went about the work of the Lord, but sadly, no. Instead I found an open row on the plane, lay down, and went to sleep. But my rest was far from peaceful. I had a horrible dream about hell and the people who are falling into the endless pit. In my dream I was startled by people saying, "Why didn't you tell me about Jesus? Why didn't you *tell me*?" I awoke from this nightmare and all was still. And when I looked around for the woman, she was gone! I hadn't noticed that the plane had already landed and all the passengers had disembarked. I hustled out of the aircraft to look for the lady, nearly leaving my briefcase aboard. I never found her. All I could think was, "What a garbage minister you are, Allen. You have time for crowds but not for real people!" I knew in that moment the Allen Griffin who was preaching on stages all over the country needed to have a come-to-Jesus meeting with the Allen Griffin who existed in private. I needed to face the undefeated sin that I preferred to keep "fragmented" away from my public persona.

I've discovered some disturbing cultures of spiritual bacteria in my life. Spiritual bacteria can only be destroyed with exposure to light and then scrubbing and washing bad habits with a potent solution of God's grace and biblical wisdom. When I brought my motivations and lifestyle to the light, I saw myself in truth. The reality of who I had become frightened me, and I resolved at that moment to never miss my opportunity again. That story is part of why I am writing this book. I won't miss this opportunity for you.

One of the most stunning revelations I experienced was that I could actually live without the benefit of a conscience. My conscience had been lost in many areas of my life, leading to my blissful ignorance of the undefeated sins I was committing more and more often. When I use the word *conscience*, please note that I am specifically talking about the power of the Holy Spirit that convicts us of our sinful acts. I lived as if God could not see the reasons or thought processes at work in my mind and heart. I would not allow the Holy Spirit to dictate what I did in the *real world*. I was thinking that in order to be successful in the world, honest, equitable worldly processes were just as valuable as Holy Spirit living. Boy, was I wrong! I tried to keep *Jesus-sy* things (did I just coin a new term?) out of my clean-cut business and social dealings, and I ultimately found myself to be double-minded and ineffective.

Merriam-Webster describes *double-minded* as: wavering in mind: undecided, vacillating; marked by hypocrisy; insincere.[1]

A double-minded man, unstable in all his ways...

—JAMES 1:8, RSV

A double minded man is unstable in all his ways.

—JAMES 1:8, KJV

How Many Versions of You Have You Discovered?

The Work You rises every day and goes to a job where you are diligent and faithful. You may arrive early and even leave late at times to accomplish your tasks on or ahead of schedule. While you are at work, opportunities are constantly being presented in which your standards of holiness are tested, but you don't see it that way. A coworker steps into your office and closes the door, then explains that the final quarter report is due. As long as you play ball and put the requisite numbers and statements together with a little bit of fluff and exaggeration, everyone will receive their Christmas bonus. Of course, you think about it for a second but then consider it a matter of camaraderie and "getting along." Any thought of integrity is lost, buried under the mantra of success at all costs.

The jokes in the conference room are as dirty as the dishes in the break room. Rather than washing the dishes for your coworkers and reminding them of your desire to be pure in speech, you just remain silent and hope they will stop. Worse yet, you let out a light chuckle and tell them they are being "crazy" or "outta control." You still haven't allowed yourself to see the moment that has been presented—the opportunity to overcome undefeated sin and even to share your faith. Instead, your office or work environment is being overrun with messages of darkness and influences of evil.

A minister once was traveling cross-country, and the man next to him had a super foul mouth. He was telling the reverend about his workplace and all that he had to do and the hard cases he had to manage. During this discussion the businessman let out a constant stream of profanity that eventually caused the pastor to speak out. The reverend asked the man if he got paid to curse, and the man replied, "No, of course not!" "Nothing at all?" asked the minister. The man then replied, "Nope, I guess it's free." The preacher then made his point: "You sure work cheap! You throw aside your character as a gentleman, inflict pain on your friends, break the Lord's commandments, and endanger your own soul—all for nothing! You certainly work cheap—too cheap!" I'll bet that businessman remained silent for the remainder of that flight!

I *never* get to do stuff like that! I never get to "stick it to 'em" and say all the right things at the right time. I usually come up with some pithy and powerful statement an hour or so after the opportunity occurs. I can then be found mumbling to myself in a corner somewhere, flashing a victory grin to myself as I pause for my brain-busting wisdom to sink into my imaginary listener. I'm the man! (In my own mind, of course.)

Being effective in the workplace is not about putting people in *their* place; it's about putting *you* in *your* place. We must be clear about who we are and what that means to those around us. When we are in the right place in our relationship with God, our relationship with man is our second and vital priority. People want to know God. They want the answers that we bring through relationship with Jesus. People do not need a shock jock attack on their lifestyle to get the clue. Everyone knows what's wrong and right; they don't need our correction. Our neighbors need to see the life of a believer demonstrated and described by the people who know and love God. The people who see you every day may have no idea that there is "another you" out there who has a relationship with God. They can't and haven't seen the Jesus side of you because you have locked it in a box called *The Church You.*

The Church You

The Church You is a frequent churchgoer, occasional donor (although you don't usually give the full 10 percent the Bible *requires*), and volunteer for the outreach programs at your church. You may find yourself attending church often, but you get disinterested if the preacher tells only Bible stories and never "applies it to you." You've become quite the church ministry "connoisseur," and you come to the services looking for a ministerial "barista"—someone who will mix the Word to your discriminating taste as one who has skimmed through the Bible enough to pass even the toughest of religious questions on *Jeopardy*.

It makes you feel good to give back, so you help with the homeless ministry. You even went on a trip once to help build a church in Haiti with a team from your local congregation. Feeling good about yourself is what it's all about. It also looks real good on your résumé! You find yourself doing more and more in the church because of the notion that God loves to see your sacrifice for Him. That's really what it is, after all...you giving up a Saturday here and there to help the homeless or visit people in a retirement home!

You think in your heart that the actions of the churchgoing busybody are what being a true believer is all about, and that God is so pleased with you that He cannot contain Himself. On the contrary, these are simply the things you have used to keep your conscience at bay and to balance out the sinister nature of *The Social You*.

The Social You

The Social You covers a great many areas of your life, and it may even have sub-personas! I know this might start to sound like a pop-psychology course at this point, but I can attest to its truth from my own experience. You make social connections at varying points in your week:

at Starbucks or your local coffee stop where you see the "regulars" and offer cordial greetings and smiles; at the grocery store where you offer fast kindness as you get in and get out; on Facebook where you connect with old buds and meet new ones; in your "entertainment zone" where you attend games or movies, participate in fantasy sports leagues, and even gaming online where you may have assembled a cast of common teammates who play with you periodically.

This social version of you has friends and acquaintances both in the flesh and online. *The Social You* has many spheres of relationships, and most of them do not intertwine, *and you don't want them to.* Why? The other personas don't agree. You would rather not intermingle these things so that you do not have to face any accountability. You don't have to live according to the standards God has set for you. You don't have to face any undefeated sin in your life. Rather, you find yourself living *in the moment* with the people around you setting your barometer of holiness.

Did you know that the target audience of online gaming by the major video-game manufacturers is not teens? The target audience is those in their midtwenties to midforties! I used to find that hard to believe until I began to play video games online with my children and discovered the ages of those playing online with us. One thing that struck me like a lightning bolt was the simplicity of access to the network of gamers around the globe. The next thing that hit me was the prevalence of profanity-laced tirades that persisted in the midst of these groups of players. Over the many years I have traveled, I have seen many so-called Christian people curse like sailors and make fools of themselves online. They never knew whom they were influencing or talking to until I entered the online gaming lounge, announced myself and who I was, and told them to knock it off! Boy, did it get silent when I rebuked people from a church where I had recently been a guest speaker.

Facebook too holds many great opportunities and uses. I find it such a pleasure to connect with long-lost friends and people about whom I have always wondered, "Whatever happened to them?" But there are some major issues with Facebook as well. Old wounds and dormant passions can be reopened. A great many marriages have been dashed on the rocks by "friendships" on Facebook. There seems to be a misguided thought that whatever we type, or text, or tweet is not *real* and therefore cannot hurt us. We somehow believe that we are living in a virtual "cloud" existence and the things that we do online remain in that cloud. This is a "What happens in Vegas" mentality, only in this case, it is a "What happens online, stays online" attitude. The enemy would love for us to remain in this world of make-believe and remain ignorant to the fact that everything we do echoes through every part of our existence.

The Truth About Accountabilty

I remember when there was a large push in the Christian world for the setting up of *accountability partners*. It seemed as if everyone was coming out with new ideas on how to maintain our integrity. I found many of these teachings to be hollow, and excuses broke down some of the best ideas and creative teachings. The truth is, we are only as accountable as we want to be. I've had a great many young men come to me and ask me to be their accountability partner, and then I would not hear from them for weeks. I had to remind them that I was there for their accountability, and they would reply, "You never called me to make me accountable!" They had it backward—and maybe you do too. Accountability that will keep us on the right track is not a spiritual policeman who watches you day in and day out and then hits you over the head with his nightstick when you fail. Accountability begins with a desire to be searched. David prayed this prayer of his own accord:

> Search me, O God, and know my heart: try me, and know my thoughts: And see if there be any wicked way in me, and lead me in the way everlasting.
> —PSALM 139:23–24, KJV

When we are trying to be deceptive and evasive, we are telling God and the leaders and authority in our life: *catch me if you can!* We don't want to come and present ourselves to the Lord and our brothers and sisters for examination, because we know that our actions require justice. Sometimes we try to defend the dark things we do by saying, "This is none of your business! What does *this* have to do with *that*?" We refuse to admit that our life is to be one continuous stream of reality. The pie chart of our life cannot be separated and rationalized. Deception will never allow honesty. We'd rather play Twenty Questions and try to elude capture as the crooks that we are! What keeps the deception of our sinful reality a secret is our unwillingness to submit ourselves for regular confession:

> Confess your faults one to another, and pray one for another, that ye may be healed. The effectual fervent prayer of a righteous man availeth much.
> —JAMES 5:16, KJV

Our lives can be confusing and at times so cluttered with a great many things. Keeping things as simple as possible will help you keep the important things of your life from being overshadowed by the peripheral. Living as ten different beings to please people whom we really should be influencing with the things of God is way too complicated and needs to be sorted out! Be the same person throughout every area of your life—a person who overcomes sin and introduces others to the Savior!

CHAPTER 3

TRAGIC TREATIES, GENERATIONAL SINS, AND CURSES

WHEN I WAS IN JUNIOR HIGH SCHOOL, I HAD a major problem. Beyond the raging hormones, pimples aplenty, and gym class embarrassments was my biggest obstacle during my two years at Northeast Middle School. Every day for about two weeks I was beaten up and my lunch or lunch money was taken. It just wasn't fair! I was a chubby little boy, and lunch was very important to me; I took exception that this individual thought they could take that culinary joy from me! (You could imagine my delight when I discovered there was a whole class dedicated to cooking! Many a time I was discovered eating other students' home economics assignments under the baking prep tables.) What to do? Fight? Nooooo! I knew better as I was way outsized and outgunned.

I finally decided that I wasn't going to take this beat down anymore. I had to get *smarter!* I came up with what I thought was a powerfully wise plan and presented it to my attacker the next day. I walked right up said, "Girl! (Stop laughing…girls were bigger than boys back then!) If you don't stop beating me up, I'm gonna tell my momma!" (My momma is no joke; she was so tough, she would spank *other people's* kids!) "Let's make a deal," I said. "I'll give you a box of Twinkies if you promise to leave me alone!" She replied, "OK!" So we had a deal! I skipped home so happy that I felt like I was floating. The only day my twelve-year-old mind could muster being this good was when McDonald's came out with super-sized food portions!

I had to find a way to purchase that box of Twinkies. I gathered up twenty-seven bottles and cans to take to the grocery store for the ten-cent deposit that Michigan refunded for each container returned. It seemed like such a bargain price for my freedom. I didn't even have to worry about an impending attack for the three days it took to gather those tokens of my deliverance. Luckily my victimizer gave me lunch-leech amnesty until that Friday when I would present to her the aforementioned bounty. With great joy and satisfaction I plunked down my hard-earned deposit slip from the turned in bottles and cans next to the register and slid my beautiful box of triumph—the Twinkies—before the cashier. With Twinkie box in one hand and receipt in the other, I emerged from Meijer Thrifty Acres victorious!

I presented the box of Twinkies to my victimizer (whose name will remain a secret to protect the *guilty*. There is no statute of limitations on acts of terror done to fat little junior high boys named Allen). I then said, "We have a deal, right?" When she replied, "Yeah, we've got a deal," I went to lunch with confidence, joy, and enthusiasm.

The sun was shining, the squirrels were chattering, kids were laughing, and I was about to enjoy my bully-free lunch. I proceeded to bite into my favorite sandwich of all time—peanut butter, marshmallow fluff, and bananas—when out of the corner of my eye I caught a figure moving fast in my direction. It was no ordinary prankster, but big, ugly bully girl number two! This girl was mean, and her breath always stunk like Worcestershire sauce...*no bueno.* She proceeded to smack me on the back of my neck, but I quickly opened my mouth and jammed my whole sandwich in. That way she couldn't get to it—but then a resounding *smack* pierced the din of the A-side dining hall. "Ow!" I cried! "What was that for?"

"I heard you're giving away free lunches!" She sneered.

"I'm not giving away nothing! This lunch is mine!"

I wish I could tell you that the girl quickly turned around and proceeded back to her seat or that one of my friends stepped in to my defense, but alas, this was my fate. She grabbed me and started slamming me on the floor. I kept screaming to my buddies for help, but for some strange reason they found what she was doing amusing! I scrambled to my feet, but my attacker pushed me and I fell to the floor. She grabbed me by one leg and was swinging me over her shoulders and back onto the floor…BAM-left! BAM-right! BAM-left! "Help me!" Security guards wouldn't even mess with this girl! I screamed for my assistant principal as he walked by. The *assistant principal* looked at the size of this beast-girl and said, "Sorry, son, you're on your own.…She's just too big and ugly!" (OK, maybe it wasn't that bad, but it seemed like it, ha ha!)

Don't Make Deals With the Enemy

I learned a valuable lesson that day: First, middle school girls are *evil*! Second, you can't make deals with the enemy. I had crossed an invisible boundary in my middle school. I didn't recognize it and hadn't figured it out at the time, but now I am older and wiser. I had caved in to the pressure of a bully and made a deal. In middle school it is acceptable to everyone that you catch a beat down once in a while, even from a girl—as long as she's much, much bigger than you are. However, what was *not* acceptable was to make a deal! It doesn't matter if you are in middle school, junior high, senior high, college, home school, or prison: if someone applies pressure to your life and as a result you cough up your goodies, you are labeled a *punk*. Then all the other bullies will come looking for you because they want a piece of the action too. I knew my fate was sealed, and indeed it was—until senior high, when…I faced her? No! When I transferred to another school district entirely. Whew!

In the same way I couldn't make a successful deal in junior high, you can't make deals with the enemy in your life! Satan will not play by the rules, nor will he give you a fair shot. He's a thief that comes to steal from you, kill you, and destroy you. That undefeated sin in your life thinks you're a punk! Sin thinks it can apply pressure to every area of your life and you will cave in to the demands and darkness it possesses. Sin applies the pressure of pornography, so we cough up a lifestyle of holiness, trading it for sexual immorality. Sin applies the pressure of gossip, so we cough up our integrity, trading it in order to spread untruth and pain. Sin applies the pressure of the crowd, so we cough up the filling of the Holy Spirit, trading it for drunkenness and revelry. Sin applies the pressure of idolatry, so we cough up security in Christ, trading it for depression and hypocrisy.

We have to treat Satan—and undefeated sin—as a hostile force and fight until we win! But all we really have to do is face our attacker and fight! "Greater is he that is in [us], than he that is in the world" (1 John 4:4, kjv). *We are not the enemy's punk!* We are *more than conquerors*! We must not only know that in our minds, but we must also put it into practice so it is demonstrated in our day-to-day lives.

The scene that I shared from my not-so-tragic middle school lunchroom is being played out before us daily. This type of encounter is described in 1 Kings 20. Ben-Hadad, the king of Syria, gathered a massive army that included thirty-two other kings of nations to fight against Israel at Samaria. These ranks surrounded the city of Samaria to besiege it. Ben-Hadad demanded that the king of Israel surrender his silver, gold, and the *loveliest* of his wives and children. To this demand, Ahab, the king of Israel, did not hesitate, but straightaway incredibly he offered them as a peace prize to Ben-Hadad! I'm so glad I wasn't part of Ahab's family! He just surrendered the lives of the royal family, without a fight, without even blinking an eye? That's exactly what I experienced in my middle school lunchroom. Ahab was too afraid to fight.

Gaining the World But...

Over the years I have noticed ministry leaders serving up their marriages and families on a silver platter, just for the opportunity to obtain success and financial gain. The pastor's kid used to be the one who paid the price. When I was growing up, people regarded the PK, the pastor's kid, so negatively. They would refer to the PK as the *most evil* of youth, and I have to admit that in many circumstances they were correct. These kids frequently did not receive the attention and care they needed from their parents, and many times rebellion was the result. It seemed that pastors were willing to ruin their children's lives and neglect their spouses for the cause of a successful growing church. That failed model of leadership eventually filtered into the congregation, and now more than ever, careers seem to take precedence over children—even in the lives of faithful churchgoers. Producing financially has become the focus, more so than a healthy marriage.

Foreclosure, bankruptcy, depression, anxiety, anger, addiction, and massive debt are real and devastating problems at times that can potentially drive us away from spiritual things. Building our business will not build a strong moral compass in the lives of our children. Networking with potential clients won't produce the atmosphere of the Holy Spirit in our homes. What's financially important does not always coexist with what is morally and ethically precious. We must not allow the hardships and struggles inherent to our society to cause us to forget what's really important. We must be even more tireless in our efforts to pastor our homes and surrender our relationships to the Lord. These relationships are not just worth defending; they are the major reason why we must fight!

Although this is a serious situation, I can't help but chuckle at what Ben-Hadad was demanding. He said that he wanted the *loveliest* of King Ahab's wives and children! That just cracks me up! Can you imagine being one of his kids after the siege? When you went to school the next day and everyone was asking what happened to your brothers and sisters, you would then tell them the bad guys had selectively stolen your siblings and their mothers. The enemy troops took all the silver and gold that was in the king's treasury, as well. Finally your schoolmates would ask you the ultimate question: "Hey—why didn't they take *you*?" Yikes! How would you explain to them you were just too ugly to be taken by the enemy marauders? That's messed up!

War historians teach that when the invading armies would come to a walled and adequately defended city like Samaria, they would place siege ramps up against the walls, doors, and windows. This would block the passage of people, animals, and supplies in and out of the city. The sheep gate, the water gate, the fish gate, the sewage gates, all would be stopped up. Essentially the city would stop all production and progress and would have to deal with the invaders. Normal life would halt, and the city would be forced to fight or surrender. Many times the enemy army would wait for the men of the city to starve before they would instigate battle so that the city defenses would be as weakened as possible. It is obvious, however, that in this case Ben-Hadad had enough forces to take the city immediately, and he didn't need to wait for any weakening effect.

Unfortunately, when Ben-Hadad received word of Ahab's decision to surrender the goods, he suddenly was not satisfied. He issued a message to Ahab that his men would then search the houses of *all* the people and seize *everything they valued*. Ben-Hadad didn't merely want *the king's* silver, gold, wives, and children; he desired the possessions of *the entire nation*. Why would he be satisfied to take just the wealthy man's goods when he could make off with the whole nation's wealth? He didn't march his armies all those miles just to get a small amount of booty; he wanted the vast abundance that Israel enjoyed. Can you see the transformation of Ahab's identity? Once he surrendered just a little bit of ground to the enemy, he became a punk to King Ben-Hadad.

Now the king of Syria would not leave him alone. If you give your enemy an inch, he's going to take a mile.

It's the same with undefeated sin in your life: give it an inch, and it will take a mile! Sin wants to rob you of everything. Darkness wants to cover the earth, and Satan is vying for a reign of infamy. Don't be naïve to the intensity of our spiritual warfare. Sin is playing for keeps. The devil's goals are bigger than your daughter becoming pregnant out of wedlock at thirteen years of age or your son being arrested for drug possession. This battle is not a battle for happiness or life fulfillment. This battle is for eternity. Sin is not simply trying to make you unhappy and depressed. Evil is not merely trying to make your life difficult. The devil, your sin nature, and evil itself are present in this world to kill you, rob you, and make you infamous both on earth and in hell. Satan wants your name to be a curse word to everyone who ever knew you, to make your name be avoided like those of Adolf Hitler, Osama bin Laden, and others. He wants to rob your today, your tomorrow, and your eternity. He is in all-out war against you!

Stop Blaming the Devil for Everything

Even with all these diabolical devices, however, many times I still believe the devil gets a bad rap. I mean it! We blame the devil for everything. If the car doesn't start...it's the devil! Can't pay my bills...it's the devil! Cheated on my taxes...it's the devil! We blame the devil for everything that ever seems to go wrong. Don't feel sorry for him, though—he does quite enough to earn his titles as liar, thief, the evil one, etc. But I can truthfully say that a majority of my own problems cannot be blamed on the devil at all. The devil is like my evil customer service manager, always giving me terrible advice and making my life difficult. But I—and I alone—am the source of nearly all of my problems. My sin nature, which gets me into trouble most of the time, is the attitude of the devil that I have carried from birth:

> Surely I was sinful at birth, sinful from the time my mother conceived me.
> —PSALM 51:5, NIV

I definitely create most of the major failures in my life; however, this does not mean there are not diabolical principalities and powers in the spiritual realms at work.

Let's get back to our Bible story. Ahab took the news back to his officials, and they immediately advised him to deny Ben-Hadad's demands. And that's what Ahab did. But upon hearing of this rejection, Ben-Hadad threatened Ahab with battle, and after exchanging the requisite prefight smack talk, it was finally time to fight. Right then a prophet showed up and told Ahab exactly what God wanted him to do in order to win this battle:

> Meanwhile a prophet came to Ahab king of Israel and announced, "This is what the LORD says: 'Do you see this vast army? I will give it into your hand today, and then you will know that I am the LORD.'"

"But who will do this?" asked Ahab.

The prophet replied, "This is what the LORD says: 'The young officers of the provincial commanders will do it.'"

"And who will start the battle?" he asked.

The prophet answered, "You will."

So Ahab summoned the young officers of the provincial commanders, 232 men. Then he assembled the rest of the Israelites, 7,000 in all. They set out at noon while Ben-Hadad and the 32 kings allied with him were in their tents getting drunk. The young officers of the provincial commanders went out first.

—1 KINGS 20:13–17, NIV

God told Ahab to take the youngest and least experienced men out to the battle to fight an army with immeasurable forces. The Israelite army was all of seven thousand troops, and the Bible describes the enemy army to be so large that they covered the countryside. Israel was outnumbered and outgunned, but as long as the Lord was with them, they were a majority. These young soldiers marched out and struck down their opponents. And after seeing such a demonstration of power from the youth of Israel, the Syrians fled and were pursued— with a great slaughter being the result.

God chose those young, inexperienced fighters for His glory. God is constantly using the weak things of this world to confound the strong. I'd bet that the veteran fighters of Israel were looking at the odds stacked against them in this fight and were thinking the same things the men of Jerusalem thought when they faced Goliath: "How can we win with such odds against us? Is our king crazy? Why didn't he just give the enemy our valuables?" The young soldiers didn't have any past experience of failure or loss. They were ignorant to such things. All these young officers knew was that their king had told them to fight and that God was on their side. They were ready to die because their king had commanded it.

Sometimes Ignorance Is Good

Are you ready to die to yourself for the cause of the King of kings? Maybe you are a veteran Christian who has seen so much failure around you, so many people mess their lives up due to undefeated sin, that you've become cynical. Maybe you feel there were times when God let you down and you are now afraid to give Him all of yourself because you don't know what the outcome will be. Maybe you have doubts because you really enjoy your life of sin, and pure Christianity appears to be an impossible task. But God's not judging you based on how you feel—only on how you respond to your feelings and fear. Stagnation is the beginning of spiritual death. You must fight if you want to kill the evil champion of undefeated sin in your life.

To change the attitudes that cause us to stagnate, we must be like the young soldiers of Israel's army. They were ignorant in battle, having fought the very least of all those in the ranks—and that was in their favor. God wants you to be ignorant to sin! He wants you to know as little as possible about the sinful things of this world—and He wants you to stay that way.

> Truly I say to you, whoever does not receive the kingdom of God like a child will not enter it at all.
>
> —MARK 10:15, NAS

God would have you come to Him as a child, ignorant of sinful things. We have been deceived by a culture that tells us we must delve into darkness in order to better help people get free of it. Then we will be able to relate to the lost and struggling. No way! That is a lie of the enemy!

> I have been crucified with Christ; it is no longer I who live, but Christ lives in me; and the life which I now live in the flesh I live by faith in the Son of God, who loved me and gave Himself for me.
>
> —GALATIANS 2:20

Leaders have come to me at times and asked me how I stay fresh and current with the trends of today and all that this generation is doing and desiring and involved in. I answer each of them with the same statement: "I don't have to listen to what they listen to, go where they go, be entertained as they are entertained, or speak as they speak in order to be relevant in their lives. They only have to know that I care, and they know that I love them when I treat them with sincerity and kindness. As long as I remain faithful to the Bible and preach the uncompromising Word of God, I will be relevant to all generations!" We must stop making the excuse of "being relevant" in order to partake in the affairs of darkness. No, we must keep our spiritual education to the level of children. If a child can watch it, read it, listen to it, go there, and participate, then so can we.

These young soldiers of Israel moved out as their king commanded, and the victory was secure—but the battle was not yet over. The prophet appeared to Ahab once again and told him that the king of Syria would return to attack him the following year. Meanwhile, the Syrian king was getting the advice from his counselors that Israel's God was a God of the mountains, so if his troops fought Israel on the plains they would win. And the prophet's words came true! The Syrians made some adjustments to their ranks and came back to once again face the army of Israel.

> The man of God came up and told the king of Israel, "This is what the LORD says: 'Because the Arameans think the LORD is a god of the hills and not a god of the valleys, I will deliver this vast army into your hands, and you will know that I am the LORD.'"
> —1 KINGS 20:28, NIV

Your enemy is convinced that your God is just the God of the *church version* of you. Your sin nature is a counter-puncher. If you go to church on Sunday and only acknowledge Jesus one or two days a week, the enemy doesn't mind. After all, he has major influence over you during the other five days of the week. He's holding all the cards, and all your multiple personas are never truly integrated to become one whole man or woman of God.

The Enemy Knows Your Seasons

Have you ever noticed that wars in Bible times were fought during specific seasons of the calendar year? If you examine your life closely, you will also see patterns of spiritual warfare and even physical attacks. At the same times of the year you may get sick, be happy, lose weight, feel motivated, or even get pregnant. At the same times of the calendar you may be tempted with sins and attitudes that are detrimental to you. The enemy of your soul may know the season you're in even more than you do! When it feels as if all hell is breaking loose in your life and the enemy is attacking you with intensity, remember that you must have a harvest of good things on the way and the enemy is simply trying to knock you off track before you can get there. You are close to your victory, so don't stop!

When you have undefeated sin in your life, your God becomes the God of Sunday services, church camps, revivals, conventions, and Wednesday night Bible studies. But after those events are over, hell is still there, waiting for its turn to strike. I've noticed I face some of my greatest spiritual battles when I am tired, and especially right *after* a great spiritual encounter. There is a propensity within me to take a little spiritual sabbatical after a great spiritual awakening. It's as if I feel I need a break from Jesus if we've spent *too much time together*. Have you noticed that you rarely feel the need to have a devotional time with the Lord on Sunday afternoons?

A great many people have scratched their heads over my next statement, but I believe it is true: *devotions are from the devil!* Wait! Don't just laugh and tell me I'm crazy; hear me out. Devotions are usually a specific time you set aside to read your Bible and pray, right? The problem arises when this process, usually a good habit, turns into a ritual and then becomes *religious*. Consider the following:

Habit: Read your Bible every day. (For the truly religious, read through the Bible at least every year—then you are *proven* to be "spiritual"!)

Devil: Read your Bible as fast as you can and treat it like you would a book report assignment, catching only those quotable precepts you can post on Twitter to sound spiritual to your friends. Then you can say to yourself, "I did it today!"

Truth: *"How blessed is the man who does not walk in the counsel of the wicked, nor stand in the path of sinners, nor sit in the seat of scoffers! But his delight is in the law of the* LORD, *and in His law he meditates day and night"* (Ps. 1:1–2, NAS).

David writes that a true believer and lover of God doesn't read the Word or study it to *know the Bible*; they read it to *know God* and grow closer to Him. Do you read the Word to know more of God for yourself?

Habit: Pray to the Lord every day. (The religious like to put a time allotment here...the more time you spend praying, the more spiritual you are. These are the people who like to tell you how long they pray every day.)

Devil: Pray every day, asking God for all the things that you want. After all, He is the interstellar Santa Claus in the sky who exists to meet all your needs and provide for all your wants. If you forget to pray, you will feel shame and believe that God has just put a strike against you. And remember: prayers before meals don't count!

Truth: *"Rejoice always; pray without ceasing; in everything give thanks; for this is God's will for you in Christ Jesus"* (1 Thess. 5:16–18, NAS)

We are to be in a constant state of communication with God. It is impossible to praise Him, love Him, make requests of Him, and seek His face without *talking* to Him! Don't miss the hundreds of chances daily to talk to the God of all creation and share your journey with Him. He cares about you!

The Bible never tells us to do these things once a day or even worship in church once or twice a week. These are acts of love that are to be performed *continually*. I am convinced that the devil himself is behind the idea of religious ritual, knowing that after a while any habit can be corrupted and then become caustic to a devoted relationship with God.

Tragic Treaty

The Israelites and Syrians only camped opposite each other for seven days during that second encounter. On the seventh day the battle began, and a huge victory came to Israel. The Israelites killed 100,000 enemy foot soldiers in one day! Israel only had 7,232 soldiers at the beginning of this battle. Each Israelite soldier would have had to kill nearly 14 Syrians apiece! That's a lot of killing for one day! God was definitely on their side. I am sure that whatever they tried to do to kill the enemy worked. One guy might have just thrown rocks, and the enemy fell as if the Israelite had shot a Tommy gun at him. Another Israelite might have had a cold, and whenever he sneezed, the enemy troops within range would lose body parts at the torrential blast of air. One very short Israeli might have just bitten the enemy on the ankle and the Syrian soldier blew up! (I know...here we go again with the fantasies, but this would make the best movie ever, and I'm going to write it just like that!)

Thousands more Syrian troops ran for their lives and hid in the city of Aphek. Then a wall collapsed and killed

27,000 more enemy soldiers! (See 1 Kings 20:30.) I will have to ask this question when I get to heaven: "How does a wall sneak up on 27,000 people?" This Bible story is amazing! King Ben-Hadad was among the troops that ran and hid in Aphek, but the Syrian king was smart enough to hide inside a building.

King Ahab was completely victorious! He had not only won the battle between Israel and Syria, but he had also defeated thirty-two other kingdoms that had joined forces with Ben-Hadad. The toils of this war would not compare to the spoils of thirty-three nations combined. While he was riding through the city of Aphek on his chariot, some men garnered Ahab's attention. They introduced themselves as spokesmen for the king of Syria, and they begged Ahab on behalf of Ben-Hadad, "Please let me live."

> The king answered, "Is he still alive? He is my brother." The men took this as a good sign and were quick to pick up his word. "Yes, your brother Ben-Hadad!" they said. "Go and get him," the king said. When Ben-Hadad came out, Ahab had him come up into his chariot. "I will return the cities my father took from your father," Ben-Hadad offered. "You may set up your own market areas in Damascus, as my father did in Samaria." Ahab said, "On the basis of a treaty I will set you free." So he made a treaty with him, and let him go.
> —1 Kings 20:32–34, niv

Can you believe that? It is hard for me to understand how Ahab could make a treaty with this man who had created so much trouble for him, even threatening him with total destruction. Ben-Hadad told Ahab earlier that he would level Samaria and that there wouldn't even be enough dust remaining for his soldiers to hold in their hands. And now Ahab was making peace and they became buddies? If this man had threatened your family with slavery and violence, would you stand together with him in a chariot acting as if it never happened? God had already told the Israelites to destroy the Syrian army that was standing in their way of possessing the entire Promised Land. Here was yet another colossal failure perpetuated by the kings of Israel.

Why did Ahab feel he needed to make a treaty with Ben-Hadad? Why settle for a treaty when the result of the military action that God has blessed had brought complete and utter victory to Israel? In a customary case the enemy nation, army, and king would have to surrender literally tons of gold and silver and pay a form of bounty for the return of their men. The defeated nation's government would also be overrun with a new leadership and demands of tribute and taxes. Israel would have conquered much, if not all, of the Promised Land that remained in enemy control at that time.

But instead of claiming his victory and possessing the land that God had promised them, Ahab *made a deal* with Ben-Hadad. Why am I making such fuss about this? Why am I emphasizing all these things and making such a big deal out of a little deal? Because this was no little deal. This deal was one of the worst deals Ahab could make. Let's take a look at what Israel and Syria agreed to in this treaty:

1. "I will return the cities my father took from your father": It appears that a former king in Syria had captured some of Israel's cities and there were still ill feelings about this. King Omri had lost Ramoth-Gilead to Ben-Hadad's father, and I am sure that city was part of the deal.

2. "You may set up marketplaces in Damascus, as I have already set them up in Samaria": The permission was granted to Ahab to set up trade zones or bazaars in the Syrian cities and regulate and police the trade without interference from the Syrian government.

In both of these situations Ahab was cheated. When you defeat an enemy army and by the power of God destroy 127,000 enemy troops, you are not supposed to get your cities back and a couple of Walmart stores! These wars were fought for kingdoms. Ahab wasn't supposed to just take a few trinkets and go home. God said that the enemy king had been given to him for *destruction*. The land was already promised to Israel; they need not give it back for the cause of peace. In fact, King Ahab and the Israeli army had just defeated the enemy under extreme circumstances, and in the end they got back what they *already owned* in this treaty! Syria was to be their possession, and the cities taken before were again their possession. This deal makes *no sense*.

Let's *Not* Make a Deal

The enemy of your soul is trying the same thing with you. The moment you begin to live free from sin and dwell in right relationship with God, that sin wants to make a deal with you. The problem with the deal is that you already have the kingdom of God, so there's nothing sin can offer you that's better than what you already own! As a believer, you already have the best life; you just have to be willing to fight for it. Your enemy is sin, and when Jesus died on the cross, He defeated sin so we could see and know it can be done. Now sin is under your feet gasping for its breath, begging, "Please let me live!" The enemy will offer you everything under the sun if you will just let sin live in you. All the enemy wants after all is a small part of you—for now. What makes this scheme even more ludicrous is the enemy doesn't even own the things he is offering. He is just a fallen angel, and sin is merely the attitude and actions of the same rebellion that cast Satan and others out of heaven.

Undefeated sin offers us popularity; all we have to do is adopt a sinful mentality and a mediocre lifestyle like that of the people we surround ourselves with. But we already own popularity. All of heaven rejoiced when you accepted Christ as your Lord and Savior. Heaven knows your name!

Undefeated sin offers us money; all we have to do is cheat on our taxes, lie on that business report, and bury ourselves in debt to prove it. But we serve a God who owns it all, and He will give it to us if we ask and are willing to be diligent and wait on His promises.

Undefeated sin offers us good sex; all we have to do is sleep around and find excitement picking up new partners along the way. But we serve the God who holds the patent on good sexual relationships. God created sex and designed it to be between one man and one woman for life. There have been tests and polls that all point to this truth: married people are the most sexually fulfilled people on the planet.

Undefeated sin offers us the party; all we have to do is mix the wrong friendships with alcohol, prescription or illegal drugs, and a general lack of self-control. But we serve a God who has the corner on the market in fun. While so many go to clubs or bars and wind up with *hangovers*, we can celebrate Jesus and live so free that we'll have Holy Ghost *makeovers*.

Undefeated sin offers you happiness, and sin *is* fun—for a while; all we have to do is sell out the One who died for us. But we serve a God who will give us joy. Joy is more than happiness and will outlast it too. Joy is not contingent upon the situations of life; joy remains when things are going well and when they are going wrong. People all over the world want joy, but so many times they settle for mere happiness.

The Cure of the Tragic Treaty

As Ahab rode away in his chariot, he saw what appeared to be a young, wounded soldier along the road who was calling to him. As Ahab's chariot came to a stop before the soldier, the tale is told:

> Your servant went out into the midst of the battle; and there, a man came over and brought a man to me, and said, "Guard this man; if by any means he is missing, your life shall be for his life, or else you shall pay a talent of silver." While your servant was busy here and there, he was gone.
> —1 KINGS 20:39–40

Ahab told the young soldier that he was out of luck; he must either pay the equivalent of seventy-five pounds of silver or lose his life. No soldier would have that kind of currency; it was more than a man's yearly wage. Then, in dramatic fashion, the soldier removed his disguise and the king immediately recognized him as one of the prophets. The prophet then pointed his righteous finger at the king and said, "This is what God says: No, *you*, King! You, O King, let a man free that God had determined should die! Therefore it will be your life for his life and your children for his children!" (See verse 42.)

A few years later Ben-Hadad would return and besiege Samaria yet again. But when Syria attacked Israel this time, they surrounded the city and forced its people into starvation. In Samaria's desperation, the price of a donkey's head was worth eighty pieces of silver and a measuring cup of doves' feces sold for five pieces of silver. The Bible describes the blight of hunger as so intense that people were boiling and eating their own children! King Jehoram and the people of Samaria were paying the price for the decision of Ahab to release the prisoner of war who now was decimating them.

No More Deals!

How many times have you complained about the terrible decisions that have been made at your workplace? Others make decisions that affect you adversely. Was your home marred by disharmony and divorce? Somewhere, someone made a deal in your parents' relationship, and it hurt you. Did you grow up in dire financial straits because of mountains of debt? At some time in your past someone made a deal that ensured financial lack and disability in your fiscal future. Maybe you wet your pillow with tears as a young person and told yourself you would never abuse your children as you were abused, nor would you allow abuse to happen. Someone made a deal and succumbed to the perversity in their sinful heart and damaged your soul. Have you made a conscious effort to avoid the missteps of your parents as they raised you? If you find yourself aligning with their past sins and failures, there is a deal for the common and comfortable resting in your hands. Somewhere in your story someone made a deal, and you have to make up your mind that the deals will stop here.

No more deals! Your journey of transformation has already begun. I challenge you: do not remain silent when the enemy is trying to destroy all that God died for in your life. Say the following out loud:

No more deals!

No more deals!

No more deals!

> Who shall separate us from the love of Christ? Shall tribulation, or distress, or persecution, or famine, or nakedness, or peril, or sword? As it is written:
> "For Your sake we are killed all day long;
> We are accounted as sheep for the slaughter."
> Yet in all these things we are more than conquerors through Him who loved us. For I am persuaded that neither death nor life, nor angels nor principalities nor powers, nor things present nor things to come, nor height nor depth, nor any other created thing, shall be able to separate us from the love of God which is in Christ Jesus our Lord.
> —ROMANS 8:35–39

What are we to do with our satanic POW—the undefeated sin in our lives? How do we respond to this onslaught of evil? I wish Ahab could have figured this out and put a sword to the throat of Israel's troubles. While the enemy is still underneath your feet, I have a recommendation: *Kill him!* Kill sin! Kill it everywhere and anywhere it is in your life, and whenever it rears its ugly head to come against you again, then kill it again! Don't give sin an opportunity to rise and bring destruction to you or to your family. This is your moment; give no place for the devil!

We must identify the evil that is among us in order to evict the undefeated sin in our lives—and that is the subject of our next chapter.

CHAPTER 4

CALL IT WHAT IT IS!

WHEN DAVID ARRIVED AT THE BATTLE, THE men had begun to rise up and shout while heading toward the battlefront. This time (after forty days) when the men saw the man Goliath, they started running for their lives! What in the world? What just happened here? The law of failure applies: do nothing long enough, and others will help you do even less. When we don't live according to the purpose of God in our lives, we will find ourselves running in the wrong direction with the wrong crowd doing the things we told ourselves we would never do. It was only a matter of time before these men would start running from the very battle that God was telling them to fight. And at that very moment Goliath became the champion over Israel.

Who is your champion? What are the things that are standing in the way of you being the man or woman of God that He is calling you to be?

Is it your uncontrolled tongue? Do you have a dirty mouth that Orbit gum couldn't even clean? I have discovered the area that seems to be the greater temptation in your life is often the very place where the Lord wants to bring tremendous victory to both you and others. There was a time when I struggled keeping my speech upright and full of integrity—and then a mentor of mine told me that my words carried weight and shouldn't be taken lightly. It was a painful process to change my bad habits, but my words needed to have spiritual empowerment, and I was willing to do what it took to experience synergy in my communication through the Holy Spirit.

Is a filthy mind holding you back? Has pornography gripped you, even as your secret sin has evaded the notice of those closest to you? Maybe you know how to erase your browsing history on the computer, and you justify your actions by saying, "They're just body parts...that's all." Sin is ravaging your sexuality, and you are living in the stupor of meaningless Internet escapades. Break free!

Are you one given to drunkenness? The excess of any one thing is wrong, but I can think of no other device that causes more harm to people, vehicles, and even good dancing than alcohol abuse. There's a reason the Bible declares, "Do not be drunk with wine, but be filled with the Holy Spirit." (See Ephesians 5:18.) The Holy Spirit cannot indwell in a person who is already filled with other things. The counterfeit peace and relaxation brought on by alcohol cannot compare to the matchless blessings of peace and joy found in the presence of God.

Is your entertainment void of positive messages and images and instead full of darkness? We live in an era where satanic entertainment is the mainstream. I recall the furor that erupted over the books and movies of Harry Potter...where has that gone? Some of the most popular books and movies today would have been deemed inappropriate and censored by many parents just a few years ago. As we have let down our guard, even darker entertainment has crept in. Are you drawn to entertainment that promotes violence? Is your entertainment ruled by destruction? Does human life mean so little to you that children can be murdered on your flat screen television and it does not affect you? If murder doesn't bother you, something's wrong, my friend.

Are illegal or prescription drugs consuming the time in your life? Do you need drugs to wake up? Drugs to go to sleep? Drugs to cope with stress? Drugs to make it through the day?

How about malicious gossip? A lot of the things we consider "sin" are so egregious that everyone would agree on them: murder, adultery, theft. But it amazes me that we do not condemn the sin of gossip as we should. Discussing the issues, problems, shortfalls, and faults of others is not merely a matter of bad taste; it is sin. The Bible does not separate gossip from other defined measures of sin. Gossip is evil.

> A scoundrel plots evil, and his speech is like
> a scorching fire. A perverse man stirs up dis-
> sension, and a gossip separates close friends.

> A violent man entices his neighbor and leads
> him down a path that is not good.
> —PROVERBS 16:27–29, NIV

Do you struggle with addiction? Addiction is an act that you cannot stop doing on your own, an action that requires intervention and divine empowerment. If there are sins that you just cannot seem to stop, you must reach out to God and ask brothers and sisters in the Lord to assist you. This is too big to fight alone!

Do you find yourself celebrating others' failures?

Are you a prolific liar?

Do you find yourself caring more about what people may think of you than God's standard of excellence?

What is that undefeated sin that is standing in the valley of your battlefield?

The Danger of Denial

One of the greatest strategies of sin in our lives is denial. In the stages of grief denial is listed as part of the process of overcoming a tragic and life-altering situation. I can tell you that sin is an eternity-shifting act that will complicate and corrupt even the most godly, fulfilled life. Sin will continue to rise in your life and push you down as long as you allow denial to take place.

Denial as defined by *Merriam-Webster* is "a psychological defense mechanism in which confrontation with a personal problem or with reality is avoided by denying the existence of the problem or reality."[1]

I have heard some of the most insane statements come out of the mouths of people regarding character and sin: "Well, she did sell drugs and steal money, but she's such a nice person." "He's got a violent temper and has been arrested for beating his wife and kids, but he was always cool to me." We can be duped into believing that sin is only real when and if others can tell we are participating in it. If we can be nice to people and put up a false front, we can pretend the sin in other parts of our lives doesn't exist.

I have never met a person who looked like a sinner. I have also never met a person who looked like a believer. You can wear all black, never shower, never smile, eat lead and spit nails, have a thousand tattoos—and be the next great world-changer for God. You can also wear sweater vests with slacks in lovely primary colors, take five showers a day, sport Old Spice aftershave, smile like a Miss America pageant contestant, eat veggies and spit rainbows, and wear a silver cross necklace dangling from your neck—and still be hell bound. It doesn't matter if your Bible has a beautiful leather case—or even has a lot of verses highlighted in it—if you don't live like that Bible teaches, you are destined for hell.

We do not want to take responsibility for our actions, and I understand why. Why would I want to face the truth? The truth hurts! I love telling the story of the shipwreck of the apostle Paul in Acts 27. Paul was a prisoner by choice and was being transported to Rome to bear witness of the love of Jesus. During the journey Paul told the soldiers and the crew of the ship to stop sailing because they were heading into hurricane season and it wasn't going to end well for them. Of course, the soldiers listened to the ship captain and owner rather than Paul (who, by this time, had sailed some thirty-five hundred nautical miles himself). No sooner had they begun making progress when a huge, hurricane-force wind struck and put them in mortal danger. The men were terrified and immediately threw the cargo off the ship. Next went the ship's tackle, and finally they gave up hope and even quit eating, figuring it was all over for them. That is when Paul stepped out on the bow of the ship, and I love the first thing he said: *"I told you!"* I love that!

> But after long abstinence from food, then Paul stood in the midst of them and said, "Men, you should have listened to me, and not have sailed from Crete and incurred this disaster and loss. And now I urge you to take heart, for there will be no loss of life among you, but only of the ship. For there stood by me this night an angel of the God to whom I belong and whom I serve, saying, 'Do not be afraid, Paul; you must be brought before Caesar; and indeed God has granted you all those who sail with you.' Therefore take heart, men, for I believe God that it will be just as it was told me. However, we must run aground on a certain island."
>
> —ACTS 27:21–26

Right after Paul made this statement, the men sensed that they were getting close to land and they begin to panic even more.

> And as the sailors were seeking to escape from the ship, when they had let down the skiff into the sea, under pretense of putting out anchors from the prow, Paul said to the centurion and the soldiers, "Unless these men stay in the ship, you cannot be saved." Then the soldiers cut away the ropes of the skiff and let it fall off.
>
> —ACTS 27:30–32

Do you know what we do in order to avoid hearing correction in our lives? We jump ship! We refuse to call out the things in our life that are wrong, and God forbid if anyone else does it for us! We'd rather jump from church to church trying to change our image and identity so that we can feel better about ourselves. This will not work. We must face the truth about who we are and what we are doing. Running away from home will not fix the problems at home. I have discovered that the people who are willing to be honest with us and tell us the things we do not want to hear are usually the people who care about us the most.

Can I be that person for you today? Don't jump ship! I know there are rats and sickness on every ship. There will always be people in the church world who are unkind and who do things that will hurt or offend you. But remember that God has you in this ship for a reason. Your church may not be the biggest ship. Your church may not be the fastest or the most beautiful ship. It may not be brand-new, like the ship on the other side of the harbor. It's not the *Good Ship Lollipop*, but it may be the place God has placed you for increasing growth. Your next dimension of victory may very well depend on you succeeding where you are. Throughout the Word people *succeeded* to the next place God had for them. If you want to move to the next place and season that God has for you, be faithful in this place. Identify what is trying to hinder you, and everything will begin to change.

You Are What You Do

Your identity is directly connected to your life choices. You are not the person you want to be or hope to be: *you are the person that you* live *to be.* My father used to instill this saying in me when I was a young man: "You are what you do." You cannot say that you are a person of integrity and passion for God while there is a sin party going on in your life. You cannot separate your actions from your persona.

In order to identify your champion, you may have to ask yourself some tough questions:

1. Why do I struggle sharing my faith with others?

2. What is my biggest temptation?

3. Do my friends and acquaintances know of my desire for God?

4. What things am I doing that I would be ashamed to tell Jesus?

There is a school of thought that instructs people to avoid speaking or thinking any negative things about themselves. They believe this will cancel the manifestation of those thoughts and words from that person's existence. I heartily disagree. If I only consider the good things about myself and do not address what is truthfully transpiring in my life, am I not living in a fantasy?

I'll never forget what a coach said to me once during a high school basketball practice: "Allen, if you work really hard on your game, you will be a solid role player in college." I will never forget those words. Every high school athlete (especially yours truly here) believes that they are going to be the next big star, and all it will take is the right sneakers or a big bottle of Gatorade. I just knew in my heart I was something special, and I set out to prove that I was going to be more than just an average starting player on a basketball team. I lifted weights, and I cut out fast food and sodas for nearly four years. I even tried special training rituals that would increase my speed and leaping ability. What happened? I became a two-time All-American basketball player for Southeastern University. I averaged eighteen points a game and fourteen rebounds a game. (Thanks, Coach Laing!) And when I look back at my performance and career in college as an adult, do you know what I was? A solid role player! I didn't receive my coach's words as the truth spoken in love. I ran from the truth. I didn't realize that the truth won't fail you, and I was deceived.

Maybe you've been deceived. The Bible tells us over and over again to humble ourselves, and we try to ignore it. We think we are destined to be superstars, and we do everything in our power to appear better than just a "good" Christian. What we fail to see is that there is only One who is great, and He's Jesus. Don't be deceived into remaining silent about your faults or weaknesses. When you begin to open up about the real you, the best honesty is obtained: self-awareness.

In our walk with Christ form follows function. If we are not doing the things that God demands, other acts (sins) will take its place. The enemy wants to give you counterfeit versions of real life in Christ.

The enemy is lying to you right now, saying you'll never be free…you'll never rise above…you'll never defeat him. But remember that the devil is a liar. If he says you can't, then you *know* you can!

PART 2

SOLUTION:
THE ANOINTING

I F YOU WERE TO WALK UP TO A COMPLETE stranger on the street and ask them what the anointing meant, they would probably look at you as if you were insane. Some might describe a dark ritual of the occult. Others might regale you with tales of kings and queens and the coronation of said royalty. But if you happen into charismatic circles, you will witness a divine reaction. People's faces light up as they do their very best to explain something they feel is nearly unexplainable. Some feel that it is the "it factor" of the ministry of the church. Some would say that the anointing is the filling of the Holy Spirit. Others would tell you how certain people "operate" in the "anointing" and then are able to do great things for God. Kenneth Copeland describes the anointing as "God on flesh doing those things that flesh cannot do."[1] I think all of our thoughts on this matter point to a divine relationship with Christ, but we can't all be correct, can we?

If we are going to live undefeated lives in Christ, we must understand what goes into the mind, body, and spirit of the victor. David defeated Goliath and so many other obstacles in his life only *after* the prophet Samuel anointed him. Only after David was anointed did he tell of slaying a lion and a bear. Something happened in David's life after his anointing. As we dig deeper into the Scriptures, we find that nearly all the powerful leaders of the nation of Israel were anointed at one time or another. What does the Bible say about the anointing? Let's dig into the natural, the supernatural, the dos, the don'ts, and the effects of the holy anointing oil, and how it can help us kick out the undefeated sin in our lives once and for all.

CHAPTER 5

WHAT IS IT?
SUPERNATURAL!

ACCORDING TO *MERRIAM-WEBSTER*, THE WORD *anoint* means to smear or rub with oil or an oily substance; to apply oil to as a sacred rite especially for consecration; to choose by or as if by divine election; to designate as if by a ritual.[1] The original anointing oil in Scripture was a recipe shared from the very kitchens of heaven. God spoke directly to Moses and gave him a compound ointment that was to be made by the artful mastery of a perfumer. This ointment was fully disclosed in Exodus:

> Moreover the LORD spoke to Moses, saying: "Also take for yourself quality spices—five hundred shekels of liquid myrrh, half as much sweet-smelling cinnamon (two hundred and fifty shekels), two hundred and fifty shekels of sweet-smelling cane, five hundred shekels of cassia, according to the shekel of the sanctuary,

and a hin of olive oil. And you shall make from these a *holy* anointing oil, an ointment compounded according to the art of the perfumer. It shall be a *holy* anointing oil. With it you shall anoint the tabernacle of meeting and the ark of the Testimony; the table and all its utensils, the lampstand and its utensils, and the altar of incense; the altar of burnt offering with all its utensils, and the laver and its base. You shall consecrate them, that they may be most *holy*; whatever touches them must be *holy*. And you shall anoint Aaron and his sons, and consecrate them, that they may minister to Me as priests.

"And you shall speak to the children of Israel, saying: 'This shall be a *holy* anointing oil to Me throughout your generations. It shall not be poured on man's flesh; nor shall you make any other like it, according to its composition. It is *holy*, and it shall be *holy* to you. Whoever compounds any like it, or whoever puts any of it on an outsider, shall be cut off from his people.'"

—EXODUS 30:22–33,
EMPHASIS ADDED

We find this anointing oil was used as a distinguishing mark of those who were set apart for God's service. One thing is for sure: this oil was to be put on people who were holy. You can't help but notice that the word *holy* is used seven times in this passage. It is quite obvious that this oil was not the traditionally used version that many people of the time used as a toiletry. This oil is special.

The people of the Bible lands would often use oil as a refresher to the face and body as the dry, dusty winds would be harsh upon the skin of inhabitants. After washing their faces and bodies, it was quite natural for the people to rub in some pure olive oil to keep their skin protected and smooth. This oil was often mixed with different perfumes and spices to add to the aroma. Anointing oneself as part of one's personal hygiene was usually abstained from during a period of mourning, and then the oil was reapplied afterward.

This common anointing was also performed for esteemed guests at banquets and before special events. The priests and Levites were first to receive this special ointment, and it was to be poured over their heads so that it dripped down their bodies. The amount of oil used for each person was not disclosed in this chapter, but other scriptures describing this ceremony show that the oil covered the men from head to foot. After the assembly of the parts of this anointing oil, there would have been nearly six quarts of oil created. Many times this ointment would be placed into a horn or flask and carried to special events and distant lands.

This oil was used to signify a transformation: from common to uncommon, from normal to special, from natural man to God's supernatural man. The people believed that there was a mysterious transference of God's essence into the life of the person who was anointed, and a connection was established between

God and man that was to be lauded and respected by all. The anointed one had the respect and admonition of the people and was a symbol of God's grace and authority evident on earth.

What's in this stuff? What exactly did God prescribe to Aaron to put in the original recipe? (Every time I write "original recipe," I can't help but think of Kentucky Fried Chicken!) There were five main ingredients in this holy anointing oil. As we study them, we will discover the recipe for our own spiritual success and the awakening of the overcomer in our lives.

Myrrh: The Painkiller

Myrrh is the first element that the Lord told Moses to put into the holy anointing oil. Myrrh has two forms that are prevalent throughout the Bible. One form of myrrh comes from the cistus plant and is in the form of a viscid white liquid. Many describe this liquid as "flowing myrrh." The second form of myrrh prevalent in Bible times was a gum resin that exuded from the bark of another variety of balsam tree. As the liquid resin seeped through the bark, it would harden as it met the air. Small deposits would then build up on the outside of the tree in the shape of teardrops. These "tears" would be reddish-brown and would then be boiled and mixed with various softening agents for use.

Most people know that myrrh was and still is utilized for its aromatic properties, and it would not surprise most of us to note it was used in the holy anointing oil for that purpose. But there's more to this story. Myrrh has other characteristics of which few people are aware. Did you know that myrrh is a topical analgesic and a painkiller? This resin could be rubbed into the skin, just like our Ben-Gay, to help alleviate aches and pains or even burns. Some forms of myrrh throughout the Bible lands today are even narcotic. Myrrh was offered to Christ right before He was crucified, to help dull the pain, but He didn't want His senses compromised and not endure all of the pain for us. He was willing to suffer the cross, with all that entailed, so that we could be saved.

When Christ was born, the Magi came from the East to visit Him. They brought special gifts for the young Jesus. Out of their treasures the Bible describes gold, frankincense, and myrrh as being given to the boy. Many Catholics believe that three kings gave the gifts and each one represented something specific. We attribute this understanding to Saint Bede, who declared that gold would represent Christ's kingship, frankincense would represent His deity, and myrrh would represent the suffering of His death on the cross.[2] With the myrrh comes the message of bitterness (the Hebrew word *more* means "bitterness"), but there is more. The characteristics of myrrh reveal a painkiller. When the Magi came to present Jesus gifts, they brought Him an aromatic painkiller. I believe what they were saying to Christ was that yes, He is our King...yes, He is our God...but also, *yes*, He is our painkiller! Jesus took upon Himself the sin and the pain of the whole world. How many times has Jesus brought you healing from your pain and delivered you from dire health issues? There have been many times in my life when I needed a painkiller, and what Tylenol couldn't fix, Motrin couldn't deaden, and Advil couldn't relieve, Jesus healed. He is and always has been our painkiller.

I was speaking at a series of camp meetings, and the Lord clearly indicated that He was going to heal the bodies of those whom we prayed over that evening. I called for the elders to come and start to pray, and no sooner had we begun than a young person came forward with a large cast on one leg. After prayer the student jumped up and down on the previously broken limb and shouted, "I don't feel any pain!" When they stripped off the cast, the young man walked with no ill effects. Later on in the week I saw him still wearing the outer protective sleeve on his left leg. I thought, "Well, maybe it was all adrenaline. I need to calm down and stop being so dramatic in altar services. I must have led this young man to believe something that never happened for him." But when I asked the boy what happened and why he was still wearing the cast, he replied, rather matter-of-factly, "Well, God healed me and I feel great, but I only brought shoes for my right foot on this trip!" Needless to say, I stopped doubting God and celebrated Jesus's healing, painkilling power in that moment.

How can you know if you are anointed? Are you a painkiller or a pain in the neck? Do people come to you with the problems and issues in their lives and you bring them relief? Not everyone has been a part of a healing miracle of a broken leg, but you can still speak words of healing into the lives of brokenhearted people who surround you every day. When Jesus arrived on the scene, everyone was looking for the man described by John the Baptist. John was a powerful man and had God-given insight about Jesus, but the way he described Christ was super-dynamic.

Picture this prophet with locusts' legs stuck between his teeth, wild honey in his beard, homemade clothing, and a gruff voice, screaming at the top of his lungs:

> You all are just a brood of vipers! And when my homeboy, Jesus, gets here, He's gonna fix all of you! You think I'm strong, I can't even untie His sandals! I now baptize people in water, but He's gonna baptize you with the Holy Spirit and with fire! [Ummm, that doesn't sound very fun to me.] He will separate the good from the evil and He will burn up the worthless like chaff! Ha!
>
> —LUKE 3:1–19,
> AUTHOR'S ADHD VERSION

John probably scared them out of their wits! When Jesus did begin His public preaching ministry, it was not extremely dogmatic, and people heard the teachings of love. Jesus and John actually had a similar message, but only Jesus brought healing. If I interviewed your coworkers, would they use a painkiller to describe how you respond to them? Do they see you as a dogmatic, raving preacher or a person who just wants their lives to be better? Jesus did not give out beatings; no, *we* hurt *Him*:

> Surely He has borne our griefs and carried our sorrows; yet we esteemed Him stricken, smitten by God, and afflicted.
>
> —ISAIAH 53:4

Jesus took the pain for us and has never stopped the transference of our sinful debts to His account. Jesus took the nature of a painkiller to another level of understanding during His arrest at Gethsemane. A group of soldiers and armed men came to take Jesus away, and then Simon Peter lashed out with a sword. (That's what I'd probably do!) He cut off the ear of the servant of the high priest, Malchus (which probably means "I can't hear you" in Greek...OK, bad joke). Jesus immediately picked up the ear, dusted it off, blew on it, and said, "Ten second rule!" He then stuck it back on the dude's head! (See John 18.) Jesus healed the very people who were leading Him to His doom. Jesus is a painkiller. Are you?

Sweet Cinnamon: The Flame of Passion

Sweet cinnamon is also used in the holy anointing oil. The text describes this element as "sweet-smelling cinnamon," and sweet is right. Those handy in the kitchen know that cinnamon is an essential element to many food preparations. I imagine this ingredient being part of the anointing oil because of its tremendously aromatic and soothing properties. Besides all of cinnamon's herbal properties, why did God choose cinnamon oil?

There is a characteristic of cinnamon that is not widely publicized in its implementation in our kitchens. Cinnamon oil is derived from the essence of the leaf of the cinnamon plant. This oil is prized for its aromatics, but also for its use in combustion. That's right, cinnamon oil is highly flammable. Why on earth would the Lord want the original anointing oil to have flammable properties? The priests were going to have to be very careful walking around those golden candlesticks if they wanted to avoid a fiery situation! Other than the wonderful scent, why would this spice be included in the Lord's anointing oil? This representation of fire seems to point toward an abiding passion.

> Passion: *often cap*; the sufferings of Christ between the night of the Last Supper and His death; an oratorio based on a gospel narrative of the Passion; *obs*: suffering; the state or capacity of being acted on by external agents or forces; emotion; *pl*: the emotions as distinguished from reason; intense, driving, or overmastering feeling or conviction; an outbreak of anger; ardent affection: love; a strong liking or desire for or devotion to some activity, object, or concept; sexual desire; an object of desire or deep interest[3]

Passion! Passion is a flame that burns at all times and cannot be put out by any normal or common means.

Fire is precious to people without stoves or self-igniting barbeque grills. Having some cinnamon oil was a great help to many people who couldn't get damp wood to light. There is much symbolism found in the presentation of this flammable and sweet-smelling spice. God's leaders are to be consumed with passion for the Lord and His precious people. This passion and heart for the things of God will then ignite others who may have become dampened by the distractions and destruction that drive our ungodly culture. There's so much to be said of a true and vibrant passion.

During the days of the Roman Colosseum, during plays and performances, it was typical for the actor to step aside for his "stunt double" (a prisoner or other undesirable person) to take the punishment or even die whenever the scene and script called for blood. Emperor Nero was famous for his use of Christians to burn, shoot through with arrows, decapitate, or otherwise destroy during these illustrated debacles. Colosseum fans felt that these killings added to the realism and made the event important because it cost someone their life; thus it became worthy of tens of thousands of revelers' undivided attention. What a mess!

There was a true passion play at work in the life and ministry of Jesus. He had passion for people! Jesus cared about the little things. He seemed to always be ready to fix the big problems that people faced, but He was just as concerned about the minutest detail. Jesus fed thousands of people with a kids' Happy Meal because He didn't want to risk the safety of the crowd by sending them home hungry. Jesus had passion, and He gave His life on the cross in demonstration of it.

One instance of passion I'll never forget took place when I watched the film *The Passion of the Christ*. I was living in Southwest Florida at the time, and our church had rented out a movie theater so that church members could invite those unsaved to see this intense epic movie about the life and death of Christ. We invited some people to join us and put them in perfectly centered seats while my wife and I moved to less desirable seats in a corner. I remember being intrigued to see what a biblical film could look like with a big budget and top-tier Hollywood actors. I was so excited about going to this movie that I forgot all about the subject matter. I was the big dummy who brought the world's largest bag of popcorn into a movie of such spiritual intensity and transformation. I completely wasted about twenty-five dollars in concessions because the opening scene of *The Passion* in the Garden of Gethsemene shut down my physical appetite and instead awakened my spirit to the sacrifice Christ made for me.

At one point during the movie the Roman soldiers were administering corporal punishment, beating Christ with bamboo rods. Every blow of those sticks was meant to break the body and will of our Savior, but instead they were breaking me. I was watching my Lord and Savior take my place and receive the punishment He did not deserve. I couldn't help but think how much of a loser I was for allowing my failures and sins to put Jesus through so much. How many times have I taken His sacrifice for granted? Tears welled up in my eyes as these emotions of unworthiness overwhelmed me. I thought, "Jesus did all this for me, and I struggle with forgiving other people, like such a pompous jerk." I had a huge lump in my throat, and I was about to reach for some water and attempt to compose myself when I heard a woman shriek from the back of the room.

"Somebody stop them! They're killing Jesus! Oh, God! No! They're gonna kill Him? Are they gonna kill Him? Somebody do something! They're killing Jesus!"

I'd never experienced anything like this before, and I probably will never again, but that entire movie theater came unglued. The house erupted in a volume of emotional release that caused every hair on my body to stand up! People were shouting and screaming out of their brokenness and hurt, and the weeping was uncontrollable. Theatergoers were heaving and sobbing, leaning up against walls and falling down to their knees asking the Lord to forgive them. I heard grown men sobbing and their backs were shaking as they wrung out every ounce of the emotion and sorrow of the moment. We were people who were beginning to understand that the price Jesus paid for us called for repentance. I cried so hard my vision was blurry and my head throbbed as I told Jesus, "I'm so sorry, Jesus....I'm sorry, Lord!"

As the many solemn scenes were reenacted before me, Christ's passionate death altered me eternally. During another scene the film showed Jesus carrying the cross up to Golgotha. The angry crowd of Jews was beating Him, kicking Him, and calling Him names. During the crowd's rejection and abuse Jesus fell repeatedly...He seemed exhausted and so very frail. I wanted to go back in time and help Him, but I was stuck there in Florida, two thousand years too late.

The din of the emotional outburst was again heard in the movie theater while Jesus carried that cross beam up the *Via Dolorosa*. My heart was so very broken and stirred...and I felt like I had to say something...do something. While Jesus was suffering with each blow of the whip and every step on that trail, I quietly began to cheer for my King. I softly prayed, "Please don't stop, Jesus! Please don't quit! Please don't call ten thousand angels to help You! Please...You can do it...You can do it! Oh, Jesus! Thank You! Thank You for doing this for *me*.... I don't deserve *You*, but I need You, Jesus!"

I know that this movie was just that—a movie. I know that this was a Hollywood actor (Jim Caviezel), that they weren't actually beating Jim, and that he wasn't really suffering. The truth is, I didn't care who played Jesus in this movie; the message of what Jesus endured had been burned into my heart for all eternity. Every time they beat Jesus's back, my family was delivered from generational curses and addiction; every time they hurt our Jesus, my mother's cancer was healed; and every time they lied about Him and called Him names, the pain of racism was washed from my heart. Jesus healed me with every ounce of suffering that He felt. Jesus paid it all for *you* and *me*!

How can you know if you are anointed? Do you have passion? I'm not talking about generalized passion for life or for your family and friends. Do you have a passion for God's people? Do you have a passion for people to know the Lord in a real way? Jesus's enduring passion was that His life would be forfeited for the betterment of all mankind. Many people say they will gladly die for their country or even their friends, but how many of us would *gladly suffer* for them? Would you be willing to face the ridicule and rejection of your esteemed coworkers and friends? Are you willing for your family members to excommunicate you? Are you prepared for people whom you like to *stop* liking you? These are some of the inherent risks that you and I face when we decide to live like those with a passion for people to know God. The moment we open up about Jesus, people will be forced to choose. We must have a passion that will allow us to burn as bright candles no matter who tries to blow us out.

Sweet Calamus: Bruised Yet Sweet

Sweet calamus is another ingredient with many uses that was promoted into being part of the original holy anointing oil. Calamus is also called "sweet flag" in various locales around the globe. Calamus is a reed-like plant that grows along the waterways in Palestine. Should you travel the Holy Land today, you will see this reed and quite possibly the small perennial flower from which the calamus essential oil is extracted. When you pick these flowers, you may be surprised to find that they exude a very subtle aroma. This significant ingredient also demonstrates hallucinogenic and carcinogenic properties when used and misused in various forms. Calamus can be found worldwide in Asia, India, the United States, Pakistan, and Northern Europe.

Questions may abound when one sniffs the specific and mild aroma of the calamus flower. Why would the God of heaven choose this small, nearly odorless, and seemingly insignificant plant flower to be used in His holy anointing oil? The discovery of the value of this plant is found within its essential oil's extraction. The recipe calls for the flowers to be picked and then placed into a pestle. The maker would then use a bristle brush or a comb and "bruise" the petals of the flower, then allow them to ferment a bit. It is only when this lovely flower is bruised that the most wonderful sweet aroma is released. After a time of preparation (bruising) and then waiting (fermenting), the plant flower is finally ready to be pressed and the aromatic essential oil is released.

Calamus is the perfect plant to use in the holy anointing oil because it best relates to the Holy One! Jesus, our Savior and Redeemer, was treated just like that small perennial flower. When Jesus presented Himself along the Jordan River and His public ministry began, it showed He had been selected for service by God. Just like that small flower, Jesus appeared during times of drought and plenty. Jesus is not a fair-weather friend. Consistency sets the calamus apart from many other flowering plants that wait for a "good time" to blossom. People took notice of this young flower that was growing in their midst. To look at Jesus, however, was not to gaze upon physical beauty. There was little reason, appearance-wise, for people to be drawn to Christ:

> Who has believed our report? And to whom
> has the arm of the LORD been revealed? For
> He shall grow up before Him as a tender plant,
> and as a root out of dry ground. He has no
> form or comeliness; and when we see Him,
> there is no beauty that we should desire Him.
> —ISAIAH 53:1–2

When Jesus began to serve, the people of Israel had been taken captive by Rome. The Israelites were constantly oppressed into an ungodly "Greek-esque" lifestyle of perversity and politics. The Word of God had been lost in four hundred years of silence from heaven and corruption by the religious leaders of the day. Jesus was a radical reformer. It must have shocked many of His rivals since He didn't look like much, yet His words were dripping with authority and Holy Spirit–given power. Even Chuck Norris would have had to bow before the obvious strength of Christ's love!

When the time had come for Christ's ultimate sacrifice on the cross, Jesus's anointing was quite evident. The Jewish leaders set up false witnesses to accuse Jesus of all kinds of things, and yet He never lashed out at them in anger. When they dragged Him before Pilate and Herod, Jesus was mocked, beaten, and abused. But at no time did Christ strike back or answer them in rage.

> He is despised and rejected by men, a Man of
> sorrows and acquainted with grief. And we
> hid, as it were, our faces from Him; He was
> despised, and we did not esteem Him. Surely
> He has borne our griefs and carried our sor-
> rows; yet we esteemed Him stricken, smitten
> by God, and afflicted.
> —ISAIAH 53:3–4

Jesus lived so much like that sweet calamus plant flower. Every time someone would rub Him the wrong way, He would only exude sweetness. I know that Jesus was anointed because Jesus was hated, despised, abused, mistreated, and murdered, but He *never* lost His sweetness. The Bible says that He went to the cross like a lamb led to the slaughter (saying not one cross word to another). Jesus only showed those evil people a heart of sweetness and loving-kindness. Jesus is love. While He was dying on the cross, He looked down at His mother and asked His beloved disciple to care for her as his own. Jesus said nothing as the insults were hurled His way from one of the thieves on the nearby cross, and yet He told the repentant thief, "Today you will be with Me in Paradise" (Luke 23:43). Jesus was caring for other people even *while* He was dying on the cross for the world! Whether He was teaching or preaching, eating at someone's home, or near death on Golgotha's hill, Jesus was the sweetest when He was being hurt. Just like that sweet calamus plant flower, Jesus showed sweetness during bruising and scourging.

But He was wounded for our transgressions, He was bruised for our iniquities; the chastisement for our peace was upon Him, and by His stripes we are healed. All we like sheep have gone astray; we have turned, every one, to his own way; and the LORD has laid on Him the iniquity of us all.

He was oppressed and He was afflicted, yet He opened not His mouth; He was led as a lamb to the slaughter, and as a sheep before its shearers is silent, so He opened not His mouth.

He was taken from prison and from judgment, and who will declare His generation? For He was cut off from the land of the living; for the transgressions of My people He was stricken.

And they made His grave with the wicked—but with the rich at His death, because He had done no violence, nor was any deceit in His mouth.

Yet it pleased the LORD to bruise Him; He has put Him to grief. When You make His soul an offering for sin, He shall see His seed, He shall prolong His days, and the pleasure of the LORD shall prosper in His hand.

He shall see the labor of His soul, and be satisfied. By His knowledge My righteous Servant shall justify many, for He shall bear their iniquities.

Therefore I will divide Him a portion with the great, and He shall divide the spoil with the strong, because He poured out His soul unto death, and He was numbered with the transgressors, and He bore the sin of many, and made intercession for the transgressors.

—ISAIAH 53:5–12

How do you know if you are living an anointed life? When people despise you, mistreat you, and hurt you, do you exude sweetness? Have you been one who maintains your sweetness at first, but then you lose it as trials and problems come your way? Is there a limit to the amount of bad treatment you are willing to endure? Whatever that limit may be, people will often push you just past the threshold of what you are willing to bear. I once heard a great statement from Pastor Jeanie Mayo: "Everyone wants to call themselves a *servant* until someone *treats* them like one!"[4] I am on a personal quest, and I invite you to join me. This is a journey to be a better man of God. I have known my fair share of Christian jerks, and I have committed in my heart that I will not be one of them! How can I assure myself that never happens? I must live the anointed life. My pastor, Jim Raley, once told of a church member who was so angry with him that bitter notes and e-mails were sent and the member was planning to leave the church for good. Knowing the principle the parishioner was so furious about was a matter of holiness and integrity, my pastor could not back down. The standard had to be maintained, but peace and kindness were still called for. Pastor Raley made an appointment with the man and sat down to discuss the issue face-to-face. The man roared and shouted, accusing the pastor of having a personal vendetta. The man attacked the pastor's credibility to a level that would cause most men to retaliate. But to the surprise of his staff, our senior pastor called for a large bowl with water and towels to be brought into the office. He then cleared the office area and began to wash the man's feet, apologizing for hurting him, offending him, or making him feel unloved or unwanted. The man was stunned. When that brother walked out of the office, he never brought false accusations or sent hate mail again.

We walk out of our anointing when we begin to defend ourselves in defenseless positions. We will be misunderstood and mistreated, but we must not allow ourselves to get into vain arguments and become distracted from what really is important. Courtrooms are full of people trying to get justice for injustices both real and perceived. So many times we want people to suffer for the things they have said or done to us. What a waste of time! By studying the lifestyle of Jesus, we see that peace cannot be legalized; it must be realized. What matters most is that people know that we love them and we want nothing more than their lives to be the best they can be. Sometimes that means we must be the doormat so that people can find the door (Jesus).

Are you anointed with sweet calamus? This has to be the most difficult part of the anointing in my estimation. Most of us are very kindhearted and accommodating, but we expect the same for ourselves through the actions of others. When other people do not reciprocate these actions and processes, it can truly cause a scene.

Most of the time we don't give much thought to our responses to those who treat us badly because we figure they "deserved it." How about when you're driving? Do you ever have road rage? I have witnessed some horrific things take place when friends and acquaintances are behind the wheel! The generosity of sweetness is one of preferring others over your rights as a human. Divine sweetness can be pretty hard to achieve in an imperfect world, but that is exactly where Jesus demonstrated His love for us...on the cross.

Cassia: Inner Cleansing and Purity

Cassia is a hilarious part of the holy anointing oil. If you are not aware of the properties of cassia, prepare to be enlightened. Cassia has only one viable function: it is not particularly aromatic; it is not a topical cure; it's not even recommended to be utilized consistently because of some inherent health risks...because cassia is a laxative! Oh, man! The jokes I would like to pour out right now would transform this book into a parody of the Exodus 30 recipe: Is God trying to get the leaders of the biblical era to be *regular*? Does God want the people to be *easygoing*? Is the power of God supposed to *flow through them* without limit? Did God think the priests were too uptight and *spiritually constipated*? Did the world need the Israelites to start a *movement*? OK, OK! I'll stop...or will I *go*? Seriously, I digress, but you have to admit, this is a very interesting inclusion in the holy anointing oil. Just like everything else in God's kingdom, this element was no accident. In fact, cassia could be the most powerful of all the ingredients added to the holy anointing oil.

Why would God choose to include this laxative in the holy anointing oil? I believe the answer lies within the nature of this potent anointing element. The cassia plant has been used throughout the Holy Land, India, and the continent of Africa to ease physical ailments, including, of course, constipation. This ingredient has been utilized by chemists in other lands such as the United States and Europe and rebranded "senna." This is a natural product that is supposed to be quite effective for those so inclined. The word *cassia* means "to split, to scrape off."[5] Cassia has been said to be able to cleanse the intestinal tract and scrub the walls of the intestines of their infections and impurities. This product is said to cleanse the body and make it more efficient and healthy.

When the holy anointing oil was prescribed to the holy men of Israel, it was to be poured upon the priests and other appropriate items described in the Scriptures. These men would then rub the oil into their skin, just as many people would in their daily skin care routine. The Hebrew word for "anointing" is *masach*; it means to daub, smear, or rub all over. You can readily see the root word where we today may derive the term *massage*. Imagine several liters of oil being poured upon one's head and allowed to flow down the hair, face, beard, clothing, and such. This oil was then vigorously rubbed into the skin. The priests and leaders believed that this anointing oil was the preparation needed to serve the Lord. They would not enter into the presence of God for worship or fulfill their duties before His covenant without this oil first being applied. This oil application was not a ritual of common cleanliness; it was a rite of passage into the deeper things of God and devoted service to the Father.

The presentation of cassia in the holy anointing oil points toward an inner cleansing and purity that God wants from all of His servants and followers. God wants a lifestyle of holiness and consecration to mark our existence. It is no coincidence that the word *holy* appears repetitively in the portion of Scripture describing this anointing oil. Holiness is not the application of an ointment, but rather the works of our living in love with God. This was no more visible than through the instruction of Christ, especially His stern rebuke of the rebellious and corrupt spiritual leaders of His day.

Jesus gave many warnings and correction to the scribes and Pharisees. These men were living a form of the rabbinical law that seemed to allow them to be adored and admonished as the premier servants of God while they lived very ungodly and unholy lives. Jesus has such a penchant for descriptive language. He describes these leaders as a "brood of vipers" and all kinds of other cool lines. Maybe we need a book of these perfect put-down lines for our next scholar party. I would just love to call someone a "blind guide," a "hypocrite," or a "blind fool" in the middle of my discourse of speech, but alas, I am not worthy of such syntax. Jesus used these words succinctly, bringing truth to the offenders as well the casual listener.

Woe to you, scribes and Pharisees, hypocrites!
For you cleanse the outside of the cup and
dish, but inside they are full of extortion and
self-indulgence. Blind Pharisee, first cleanse
the inside of the cup and dish, that the outside of them may be clean also. Woe to you,
scribes and Pharisees, hypocrites! For you are
like whitewashed tombs which indeed appear
beautiful outwardly, but inside are full of dead
men's bones and all uncleanness. Even so you
also outwardly appear righteous to men, but
inside you are full of hypocrisy and lawlessness.
—MATTHEW 23:25–28

It is very clear, in this instance, what Jesus is
describing. The Pharisees and scribes had a talent for
making life difficult for the common man. They desired
to be seen as powerful and influential as they brought
the teaching of the Law to the people. Often they would
distort the truth to put a great burden on the people and
make themselves look holier and even more pious. These
men followed extreme versions of the teaching of the Law
and would harshly chastise anyone who would oppose
how they interpreted scripture...but even more so a
Christ who would come and speak an understanding of
the Law that would set men free from extreme religious
rites and rituals. They taught the practice of "extreme
washing," and in some cases would be seen washing their
hands up to fifteen times a day! Jesus pointed out that
this extreme cleansing could not make a difference in
the lives of these men or others if the purity was only on

the outside. Jesus told the people that unless they were cleansed from the inside, nothing on the outside would make a difference. To only look like you are anointed is not to be anointed. The anointing must be supported from the inside of a person, not the application of ointment and the recitation of religious prayers.

Jesus summed up all the Law and the prophets with the statement: "Love the LORD your God with all your heart, with all your soul, with all your strength, and with all your mind" (Luke 10:27). Then He added that we should love our neighbor as we love ourselves. This requires holiness, and the holiness behind love is not merely an outward expression of piety and honor. It encompasses an internal struggle that must be won for the sake of relationship. God knows our thoughts and intentions. He is then able to judge these and hold us accountable for them. If we have an outer appearance of godliness, and yet behind closed doors we refuse to live out that godly persona, we are not believers at all, but fakers and imitations. The anointing will not abide within and upon an unholy vessel. Jesus wants us to be clean from the inside out!

I know that Jesus was anointed because He lived a holy life. He was tempted and tried in every manner of sin, and yet He withstood the opportunities to fail, and He never gave in to impurity. Jesus was tempted by Satan himself, and yet He was able to maintain the standard of holiness to which we all ascribe today. Many people will say that the devil is coming against them and even, "The devil made me do it!", but the truth is that *we* are the greatest hindrances to our own spiritual success. Most of us fall into sinful actions on our own; there is no devil anywhere to be found! But Jesus was not tripped up by His own temptations from within, nor the ones brought to Him by the presence of Satan.

How do you know if you are anointed? Do you live a holy life? I'm not talking about the formulaic repetition of religious rites, rituals, and roles. Far too many times we imagine the things of God and the power of God are reserved for those who live in utter and total perfection, and we believe that the Lord is basically angry at us all the time. God is not mad at us, and He's not watching us, just waiting to remove His love and presence away from us for some mistake or dumb act that we have committed. Holiness is more than trying to be perfect. Holiness is comprised of the acts of love that spring from a life committed to pleasing God.

When I was in college, I had a crush on a woman whom I desperately wanted to impress. I remember taking her out on a date, and although there were several other people with us, I felt like we were really connecting. When we walked into the movie theater, I stepped up and paid for both tickets. (Now you *know* I liked her…I *paid!*) Then I asked her if she wanted anything from the concession stand. She said, "I'll just share with you."

"Ohhh," I thought, "this is it! She wants to share popcorn with me!" This was a huge step in our budding relationship. I decided quickly that I would buy just one bag of popcorn and one drink. If you buy only one drink, you can always put two straws in it so your date doesn't find you presumptuous. Then as the movie progresses, you can push down one of the straws, so that soon you're drinking out of the same straw. I imagined that if she didn't complain about sharing a straw with me halfway through the movie, then she must have some kind of feelings for me. One bag of buttered popcorn is also a recipe for dating success. Buttery, salty fingers reaching for popcorn *have to* touch when there is a *shared* bag of popcorn. I had this whole dating thing worked out and was well on my way to a victorious premarital hand-holding and spit-swapping session at the behest of extra-buttery popcorn and the longest soda straw I could find. After all, sharing a straw is the same as kissing, right?

All my friends thought I had to be *the man* to get this young lady to go with me to this movie. I was the envy of many guys from my dorm as I had the "perfect date" set up. But not long after the movie started, I noticed my date getting a bit uncomfortable, so I asked her if she was OK. She said she was fine, and we went back to sharing popcorn. About halfway through the movie, she excused herself and went to the bathroom. Mid-movie restroom runs are not unusual for a girl. What was unusual was that she left the theater alone. Girls never go to the bathroom alone! Solo restroom ventures go against the divine sisterhood of the tiny bladder. I began to get more and more nervous as it took her longer and longer to return. Finally one of my friends looked back at where I was sitting and said, "Man, your girl left you!" I laughed it off and wondered how she could do that to me. I was well groomed, well mannered, and stunningly handsome (kinda). Where was she?

I left my popcorn and soda sitting there and went out to the lobby to look for my date. At first I couldn't find her, but soon her activities were made known to all. I found her at the end of one of the long hallways near the opposite end of the building—nowhere near the women's restrooms. She was sitting on the floor with two girls, talking. I walked up, and I was not happy. I had bought her tickets and concessions, and she was sitting there hanging out with some friends instead of enjoying the handholding and straw action I had orchestrated? The rejection was more than I could bear, so I reacted like a hurt puppy, walked over, and said, "Hey, where have you been? I was look—" She immediately put her hand up as if to silence me, and then she started talking to the girls again, motioning to me that they would be a few more moments. "Oh! She thinks I'm just gonna sit here and wait like that, huh?" (Well…I did.)

When she finished talking to the girls, they began to pray, and she invited me to join them. We prayed for what seemed like an eternity. The two girls were crying, and my date was beaming with joy. I was miserable. I didn't understand what was going on, and I was still upset about my date investment that had gone up in smoke. When she finally said good-bye to the girls, she turned to me and spoke first: "Allen, I'm so sorry I left the movie.…It's just the movie wasn't *me*. So I came out in the lobby and I saw those girls and I felt like the Lord wanted me to encourage them and share His love with them. You know Nicole, she goes to our church once in a while, but the other girl, Margaret, she just accepted Jesus as her Lord and Savior for the first time! Nicole rededicated herself to God too! I'm sorry we missed the movie, but this was the highlight of my week!"

My date and I talked a lot more after that, but I don't remember much else of the evening. All I could think of was the statement that she made: *This movie just wasn't me*. I walked her to her car in the theater parking lot, and she hugged me and thanked me for a great time. I walked back toward the movie theater thinking I should just go in and finish watching the movie when I noticed the theater sign. The movie wasn't rated R or even PG-13. So what was wrong with it? Unfortunately I was asking the wrong question of myself. I should have asked, "What's right with it?" I stopped on the curb of the movie theater and sat down. I couldn't help but be jealous of her relationship with God, and I began to pray, "Lord, what is it that's in me that allows me to watch this movie, but another one of Your children would say it is darkness? Whatever is in her…I want it! I want to be offended at sin no matter what the rating!" Holiness is neither legalism nor competition; holiness is matrimony. The question may be, who among us will be the *treasured* bride?

Since God is the eternal Groom and I am the bride (man…I'm an ugly wife!), this relationship must take shape in a linear fashion. When I got married to the love of my life, I didn't immediately transform overnight. I continued loving my wife and living to please her. My actions continued to develop, and I began to act more and more like a married man. It took some time, and I wasn't perfect, but I am in love. Our relationship with God is the same way. We are to be committed to love Him and live to please Him. We have no idea what this relationship is all about or what the deep ramifications are until we have been committed for some time. Our goal in living a loving existence for God is to please Him daily and eternally. Religion fails holiness because religion says that if I do the same things over and over and I look like I care about you on the outside, my heart can wander and be hidden in any impure agenda I desire. Imagine every time your wife kisses you, she's imagining her old boyfriend from years ago. If you knew it was going on, you would be understandably bothered. God knows what you and I are thinking, and it bothers Him when His bride hasn't given Him her heart, soul, and mind!

Do you live committed to pleasing the Lord every day of your life? Is pleasing the Lord more important to you than anything else that would please you? If this is the case, then holiness is your natural reaction to your heavenly Groom and you are living in His favor.

Olive Oil: Central to the "Right Now" Anointing

The central ingredient used in the holy anointing oil is olive oil. Olive oil is used extensively today, just as it was during the era of its assignment. Olive oil is the perfect suspension for the essential oils and scents of the other four ingredients.

Olive oil is a relatively volatile oil. When kept sealed, the oil will last for quite some time without spoiling, but much of the taste and healthy fats degrade. Olive oil is best if utilized immediately. Olive oil has many healthy and beneficial properties, but outside of its natural and lukewarm state there are drawbacks. When used in frying, much of the olive oil's base goodness can turn carcinogenic. Consistency is the key to this element enduring and making an impact.

Why would God choose this sensitive and yet common liquid to hold and convene His holy anointing oil? Because of the sensitivity of olive oil, it was often used as a daily toiletry in the lands of the Mediterranean. Homer called olive oil "liquid gold."[6] Many of the ancient Grecian athletes would rub it into their bodies to make themselves look stronger and better. This oil would make that which was unpliable and unhealthy come alive and function as fresh and new. Daily application was the norm in such dry and windy lands. The same is true of God's anointing for His people. Through an intimate relationship and life of love toward Him, we are to be submitted to Him daily and live out the life of a servant. God will take lives that appear dead, dry, and lost and bring them to refreshing and renewal of life.

Have you ever smelled or tasted rancid olive oil? Olive oil will spoil if too much is procured and not all of it is used. We are all given supernatural ability to impact our world. To be stagnant and unmoving is to waste our oil. Our anointing is for now. We must do something now for the Lord. He will refresh us daily, but we must use the oil or we will not be able to be refilled. Our vessels will then be spoiled with old missed and misused opportunities. Many people run to conferences and conventions, chasing spiritual leaders, hoping to get their "anointing." While impartations of God's leaders are available and possible, what about tomorrow or the next day? How can you live in the anointing on a daily basis? The anointing that God wants for your life comes through relationship, not merely a momentary touch. The anointing causes us to become more dependent upon the Lord and others in relationship.

Olive oil has some interesting uses and properties that also explain its use in the holy anointing oil. Olive oil can be dropped into the ear canals to loosen ear wax that would clog and inhibit a person's hearing. The anointing makes us more sensitive to the voice of God and the needs of people. You don't need excellent hearing to serve yourself and meet your own needs. Our hearing must be sharp in order to serve those who are crying out for help and love. Olive oil was also used in certain mouthwashes for dry mouth, bad breath, and persistent coughs. I find it interesting that the base element for the anointing will influence and enable more effective communication. The anointing of God enables us to be influential communicators and will soften our harsh and dispassionate speech.

Olive oil has been utilized in the creation of the modern semiconductor. Maybe you thought it had no technological benefit. Semiconductors are valuable to the efficiency and speed of postmodern era electronics and computerized devices. You can thank olive oil for playing a part in the development of the processors used in your precious smartphones and flat-panel video displays. Most would agree that we'd be lost without our modern techno-conveniences. But we would be *truly* lost if the anointing were eliminated from our existence. This element of olive oil reminds us that we must be efficient conductors of the kind of life that God desires. As olive oil has assisted in the transfer of electrical impulses, so we must have the very pulse of God, responding to what His heart is directing us to do. We are the techno-device in His hand. We must remain a conductor or be doomed for a hardware crash (for you non-geeks: we must respond correctly to God's input or our lives will eternally fail).

I know that Jesus was anointed because the characteristics of the olive oil were at work in Him daily. Jesus is the picture of consistency and efficiency. Jesus would preach the gospel, feed the people, heal bodies, affirm the downtrodden, defend the weak, and convict the insincere...all in a day's work. He would often pray through the night, receiving all that His Father had for Him, so that He could give us more the next day. Jesus's words were unique but weighty with eternal truth and biblical doctrine. Jesus used modern terms, but He quoted the Hebrew Scripture with an authority and a passion that could only be gained by intense study.

How do you know if you're anointed? Are you walking in a spiritual consistency with God? Can others sense that your words are weighty with the love and compassion of God? Do you hear the needs of others in your daily routine, or is the majority of your life and time spent taking care of yourself? Are you willing to let those in authority over you impact the aroma of your thoughts and actions? We have all heard the statement: he or she is "too heavenly minded to be any earthly good." I take issue with that statement. If we are heavenly minded, we will have more earthly impact and good influence than anything in creation! To be heavenly minded is to be kingdom focused. To be kingdom focused is to be caring and compassionate. To be caring, compassionate, sensitive, and observant is to be like Christ. No wise person would ever say that Jesus was not any earthly good! Jesus saved the world!

CHAPTER 6

WHAT THE ANOINTING IS NOT

THROUGHOUT MY YEARS OF CHURCH attendance I have heard people use the word *anointing* or *anointed* for nearly everything! I remember sitting in church at the Community Bible Baptist Church in Grand Rapids, Michigan, and hearing a song performed by a group called the Ambassadors. Immediately after the song had ended and the crowd had said "Amen," a woman leaned over to my mother and said, "That song was so anointed." I was eight years old at the time, and I remember thinking, "What is that?" Later on I heard the same thing at First Assembly in Grand Rapids, Michigan, as my pastor described the preaching of a coming evangelist by saying, "His preaching is so anointed." In a United Methodist church in Battle Creek, Michigan, my then-pastoring brother was described to me as "anointed." During times of ministry in altar services in churches all over the country, people would tell me that my singing was "anointed" and that my preaching "had the oil." I can tell you that I really had no idea what these people were talking about. I simply thought that "anointed" meant that those people felt like what I was doing was a good thing and they wanted to encourage me to continue.

Anointing could be one of the most misused and abused words in all of Christendom. I have heard people say, "That fried chicken was anointed!" and I guess it was since it was dipped in oil...right? There was a time when I was traveling with an international evangelist and was serving and singing during his revivals. During this particular time in my life I was struggling with a time of questioning God's love for me and my faith was shaky. I was experiencing what I later described as a dry spell, in which I had been led out into a spiritual desert to become more dependent upon the Lord and not on my emotions or feelings. I continued to pursue God during this time, but I remember having so many questions and times of rebellion against God's will for my future.

Taltented: Gifted but Not Anointed

During one period of rebellion, I was singing in a church revival service. I was struggling in my walk with God and was asking Him if I was truly at liberty to serve Him or turn away. It seemed that when prominent Christian leaders made mistakes, all the world would turn on them and crush them. The treatment of people who'd done some wrong things scared me. Was I just

God's ministry robot? Was He to wind me up emotionally and I was supposed to run and run and never get tired or mess up? I thought that if I did fail, He would just throw me away like a broken toy. I later discovered that the way men react to failure is not the way God sees the situation. People can be very cruel, but God is always faithful and kind. I judged God through my own eyes and not the Word. Indeed, that was the problem. I hadn't been reading the Word and being consistent in the tenets of my faith.

While I was singing a song during that church service, I was literally in the middle of an ongoing argument with God. My twenty-one-year-old mind was so distracted I wasn't focused on my vocal performance. Suddenly, with a loud shriek, one of the women from the church jumped to her feet and began whooping and hollering and jumping up and down! I was like, "Oh, no! Here we go...crazy church lady alert!" I really just wanted to finish the song, sit down, and continue fighting with God over the rebellion in my heart, but I knew something was going on in the life of that woman. My curiosity was beginning to win out over my jaded pessimism, so I remained at the microphone as the song ended.

The pastor was trying to talk to the emphatic woman and soon had the information he desired. He then bounded up to the front excitedly and began his celebratory announcement with the statement, "Brother Allen, that song you just sang was so *anointed!*"

"Ugh! Seriously?" I thought. "Because I really don't even want to be here right now! I am even struggling with the very existence of God and you're telling me I am anointed?"

He continued, "While you were singing that song about the miraculous power of God in our lives, this woman's cancerous tumor dissolved and disappeared. She was going in for surgery very soon, but the whole volleyball-sized mass is gone!"

Everyone started clapping and praising God. That church erupted with joy and emotion that could not be denied. It was some time before we could even continue addressing the congregation. Pockets of worship would break out in the audience, and then everyone else would again join the weeping, singing, dancing, and shouting.

While everyone else was thrilled with the news of a miracle taking place in their midst, I wasn't happy at all. I even thought, "This isn't right! How can someone get healed when I'm this miserable? Stop clapping, dumb people! Nobody should get healed right now! I'm not even right with God!" I didn't understand what was going on. How was I *anointed* through all my selfishness, pride, and sin? While I did not understand that I was being used of God, that did not mean I was necessarily *anointed*.

The song I was singing that night lyrically contained direct portions of Scripture about God's miraculous works. I was singing the Word of God, and the *Word of God* was anointed, not me. It wasn't my singing after all; it was *what* I was singing that made a difference.

Hearing the Bible activates faith. As I was singing the Word of God, faith was ignited in that physically broken woman, faith enough for her healing.

> So then faith comes by hearing, and hearing by the word of God.
>
> —ROMANS 10:17

Soon after that encounter in New Jersey I found a deeper understanding of God's holy anointing for my life. I went on an extended fast. I wanted to hear God's voice and direction for my life, and I was hungry for more. After several days of eating nothing and only drinking water, I felt like I was propelled into a spiritual awakening. (By the way, you may want to avoid exercising during a fast...dizziness almost got me run over by a car while jogging!) The Lord began exposing a lot of the things in my life that had derailed my relationship with Him and had placed me in lukewarm mediocrity. I had gotten into a pharisaical repetition of religious rituals and had forgotten about simply loving God. This departure from what had become rote rekindled my divine romance.

You may think that the anointing is evident by someone's supernatural gifting or talents. If there's a major lesson I have garnered from thousands of powerful encounter services while preaching all over the globe, it is that gifting and talents are *not* the anointing. Many of us have witnessed church leaders who have major character flaws and sin issues at work in their lives. During times of ministry it is easy to confuse God's miraculous works and the gifts of the Spirit with the anointing. I have known ministers who performed miracles and prophesied life-altering events and situations with remarkable accuracy and yet were living in moral chaos. A believer may think that holiness is the requirement for God to use any man or woman, but history and Scripture show that is not always the case. While holiness is a key to faithful service to the Lord, we know God can use anyone, and He often does.

Balaam was a powerful prophet in the Old Testament, but he began to disobey God's directives for his life and started prophesying for profit. Balaam was on his way to a prophecy gig where he was to be paid to curse the children of Israel. For an unforeseen reason his donkey stopped dead in its tracks and refused to move. After three successive stoppages to his journey Balaam grew extremely frustrated with his animal and began to beat the donkey mercilessly, even threatening to kill it. Miraculously the donkey suddenly began to speak! The donkey asked Balaam, "Why are you beating me?" The prophet and the donkey then began to have a conversation about loyalty. The Lord then gave Balaam spiritual sight, and he saw an angel standing in the road with a sword drawn to kill! Balaam was warned to obey God no matter the cost in this world.

We know that God used Balaam's donkey for a powerful and poignant lesson. The power of God moved upon this donkey and directed her to know when she was heading a direction that God did not want her to go. She also spoke as the Lord gave her what to say. I've never met a talking donkey, but I would guess this donkey was special! Just the same, there are many "spiritually elite" people who are no more anointed than this donkey. To be used by God is not the same as being in an eternally significant relationship with Him. God uses many, many people, but not all people are in *love* with God.

> Not everyone who says to Me, "Lord, Lord," shall enter the kingdom of heaven, but he who does the will of My Father in heaven. Many will say to Me in that day, "Lord, Lord, have we not prophesied in Your name, cast out demons in Your name, and done many wonders in Your name?" And then I will declare to them, "I never knew you; depart from Me, you who practice lawlessness!"
>
> —MATTHEW 7:21–23

The anointing does not necessarily include demonstrations of spiritual gifting or magnificent and miraculous feats. The anointing is not a great performance or a flowery presentation of the gospel that inspires. The anointing is not what causes some prayers to be answered and others seemingly to be ignored. The anointing is not that *thing* that makes one person "better" than another in God's or man's eyes. The anointing of God is bigger than all of these things, and it's central to all that really matters in the life of a follower of Christ.

CHAPTER 7

WHAT DID JESUS WEAR?

E KNOW THAT THE PROPHETS, PRIESTS, and kings were anointed with special anointing oil that marked them as set apart and holy unto the Lord. But what about Jesus? While we know that He lived an anointed life, was He ever physically anointed? Jesus *was* anointed, but not in a manner befitting His stature, nor by one that the elders would esteem as worthy of the honor. Jesus was anointed by one of His female disciples, Mary.

Jesus was invited to the home of a man named Simon the Leper. Many theologians believe that Simon had once been a leper and was healed by Christ. They claim that is why his home was about two miles outside of Jerusalem, in Bethany, where lepers were permitted to reside. Other theologians have asserted that Simon could have also been excommunicated from the synagogue for other reasons and therefore been deemed "leprous" as a follower of Christ's sect, called "The Way" at that time.

While Jesus was reclining at the table of Simon, Mary came in and broke open a jar of very expensive perfume, then poured it on Jesus's head. This female disciple had quite the knack for the dramatic and the spontaneous. Mary had been a consistent and constant servant of Christ from their first encounter, and now she honored Him with a very precious gift. And Mary didn't stop at anointing Jesus's head. The Book of John shows that she also anointed His feet with the precious oil and wiped His feet with her hair.

Broken Devotion

The oil used in this emotional scene to anoint the head of our Lord was Himalayan spikenard, also referred to as Indian spike. The plant from which this oil is derived has many hairy spikes coming out of one root. The extracted perfume from this plant is actually quite lovely. Powerful and wealthy Romans used spikenard to anoint political heads of state, major leaders, and even kings.

The jar containing the precious ointment gives us wisdom on Mary's heart toward Christ: broken devotion. That alabaster jar held very expensive oil and was usually reserved by a woman for the most important days of her life. Many women would save valuable perfumes and oils for weddings and other major life celebrations. These perfume jars had to be broken open to be used. Once opened, they were to be used all at once and none of the perfume wasted. Once opened, alabaster jars could not be stopped up or closed again.

Mary's love for Christ was one of brokenness. She had torn away all exterior appearance of self-reliance. There was no part of her life left unsurrendered to God's will. She broke open that which could not be restored and regretted not one moment in giving Christ the most valuable gift He could receive at that time. Mary gave Jesus the kind of devotion that Jesus's passion requires. Do you have that kind of devotion to your Lord? Do you recognize Him for the superhero that He is and give Him the kind of reception worthy of His excellent greatness?

What really blows my mind is the insensitive and obnoxious response of the other disciples in the room during Mary's offering. The Scriptures describe the disciple's attitude as *aganakteō*, which means they had a "violent irritation, physically."[1] I would say that is pretty serious; it could be imagined that these men said: "That is disgusting!" "That is uncalled for!" "That is just too much...you're way out of line, woman!" Or even, "You've gone too far this time, Mary. What's wrong with you?"

The disciples were indignant, and the first one to step up and complain, of course, was Judas. He was the disciple who held the moneybag, and the Scriptures even tell us that he was a thief and would help himself to the Master's cash at his leisure. What a hypocrite! But Judas was not alone in his response to Mary's anointing of Jesus. Matthew 26 tells us that the other disciples felt this way too, and they voiced their displeasure saying:

"Why this waste? For this fragrant oil might have been sold for much and given to the poor." (vv. 8–9). Judas chimed in to inform the others that the value of the oil was established at an average man's year of wages. Judas was called the "son of perdition" by Christ, which means the "son of waste," so I guess he would know best, huh? Can you imagine the audacity of these men to complain about the value of the oil that Mary had lovingly and sincerely poured upon the head of the Savior? She didn't pour valuable oil on her boyfriend, her husband or fiancé, some famous athlete, or even her own father. Mary poured her love on the one Person who *is* worthy of all the glory and the honor and the praise!

It is offensive to me to hear the disciples speak so harshly about this kind of honor being bestowed upon the Lord. How could they feel this way? After all, they had now been with Him for years, traveling throughout the land, healing the sick, raising the dead, casting out demons, feeding the multitudes, and changing lives for eternity. How could they still not understand? How could it be that the woman who couldn't even sit at the table and eat with Jesus (because of cultural restrictions) actually knew Him best?

Pour It All Out

Some of us who have been in the church world our whole lives can become blinded to the light of God's love and mercy, and we forget that we are nothing without Him. We begin a journey toward arrogance, believing that God is worthy of whatever amount of devotion we decide to give Him from our overcomplicated lives.

Somehow we feel that God should be satisfied with our halfhearted, lukewarm affection. It's easy to get caught up in living a lie but lacking true passion for the Lord. Living lives of self-righteousness like the Pharisees, of overcompensating spiritual-image whoredom like the scribes, and of a vicious money love triangle like the lawyers and Sadducees are some of the greatest temptations of our time.

Just as Mary's cruse of perfume was either open or closed, broken or whole, we are either totally surrendered to the will and purpose God has for us or we are not. There are no resealable containers of commitment to Christ. We must renew ourselves daily in relationship to Him, or else our devotion will run dry or spoil.

Mary poured that valuable oil on Christ because she knew who He was! Maybe to some of the disciples Jesus was just a carpenter and a good man. Maybe to a couple of guys Jesus was viewed as a leader of a great rebellion that would turn them all into political heroes through victory over Rome. I'm sure some of the disciples imagined Jesus was the greatest prophet to come along since Elijah, and therefore He was a great person to follow. No matter what these men were thinking, none of them seemed willing to acknowledge who Jesus really is: the King. But when Mary poured out that perfume, she made a very powerful statement to Jesus, and Jesus explains it boldly to the disciples:

> But when Jesus was aware of it, He said to them, "Why do you trouble the woman? For she has done a good work for Me. For you have the poor with you always, but Me you do not have always. *For in pouring this fragrant oil on My body, she did it for My burial.*"
>
> —MATTHEW 26:10–12
> EMPHASIS ADDED

What did Jesus mean? Why would He say that she had done it for His burial? Was spikenard something that the people commonly used on those who were being buried or embalmed? Himalayan spikenard was a very expensive and exclusive product. It was not commonly used as a balm for burial or embalming, but neither was it uncommon for it to be poured over the brows of kings. Some scholars believe Jesus was referring to this anointing as preparation for His death on the cross, but there is more to it than just that. This oil was used by the very elect in Rome's cultural circles. This was the anointing oil of the Eastern kings. After Mary anointed Christ, He even *smelled* like a king! She confirmed what we today know and readily praise: Jesus is our King.

In a Roman republic kings were not common. Herod was allowed to reign as king over a small region under the supervision of the Roman Caesar Augustus. These so-called kings were only permissible as long as they bowed their knee to the authority and godhead of Caesar. Jesus now had the anointing that the kings would wear. The only fault that seemed to stick in the minds of the leadership of this small province was that Jesus supposedly claimed to be a king. When Jesus was hung on that cruel cross, the crime that they affixed to that tree above His head was "Jesus of Nazareth, King of the Jews." They killed Him for His kingdom. They would not allow any other kings but that of Caesar; bow to Caesar as a god or else. Jesus's aroma was further proof that He was who they said He was. Mary poured the death penalty on Christ, but she was the only one who seemed to know who Jesus truly is...not just any king, He's the King of kings! Not just a wealthy landlord, but Lord of all lords!

CHAPTER 8

OIL CHANGE—
HOW TO GET IT

THERE ARE AS MANY SERMONS ON HOW TO attain the anointing as there are statements made about people who appear to have it. Some leaders whip up miraculous potions and prayers that will supposedly draw you closer to the throne room of God where the precious holy anointing of God's favor and blessing will fall upon you. Other communicators promise us that if we send in the right amount of money, they will send us a remnant or a relic that will carry some form of blessing of anointing within. I would love to tell you the anointing could be bought for a fifty-dollar donation because that would be the easy way of receiving this holy blessing from the Father. But if it were true, billionaires all over the world would actually *own* God's anointing!

No, from all indications in the Bible, there is only one way to be anointed today—and that is to serve.

No one can proclaim over you what true devoted service can afford you. I wish I could just make appointments with all the world's greatest ministry leaders and have them pray and lay their hands on my head, and then I would gather their anointing from God. That would be incredible! I would then assemble the most powerful qualities of these heroes as a DNA plan for world domination: the preaching ability/insight of T. D. Jakes, the appeal of Joel Osteen, the authority of Rod Parsley, the prosperity of Kenneth Copeland, the humor of Jesse Duplantis, the teaching of Derek Prince, the motivation of John Bevere, the prophetic teaching of Perry Stone, the healing ministry of Benny Hinn, and the influence of David Yonggi Cho! Wouldn't that be incredible?

Now...if I could only find a preacher who has the anointing to fly, my superhuman DNA would be complete! I would then be able to walk on water, let my shadow heal the masses, pray down fire from heaven, and raise dead people back to life!

Acquiring the powers of the prophets seems like an impossible and laughable task, and it is. Too many of us roam the spiritual television networks and webcasts looking for a new teaching that we may devour, teaching that contains the access codes to the promised life. If we could only subscribe to the broadcast channel of heaven, we'd understand how God's holy anointing can be received.

The kingdom of God is the basis for understanding the acquisition of God's anointing for your life. When we try to understand and follow the leadership of Israel's government and the kingdom of God, corruption can occur. Our knowledge of the way God's rule works in our lives is often twisted by our individual understanding of government. My friends who reside in democratic societies often visualize the things of God through the eyes of this form of government. But problems arise because God's kingdom is a *theocracy*. We don't get the opportunity to vote on God's directions or plans for our lives. We either obey Him or we disobey Him.

> Seeing then that we have a great High Priest who has passed through the heavens, Jesus the Son of God, let us hold fast our confession. For we do not have a High Priest who cannot sympathize with our weaknesses, but was in all points tempted as we are, yet without sin. Let us therefore come boldly to the throne of grace, that we may obtain mercy and find grace to help in time of need.
> —HEBREWS 4:14–16

Have you ever heard people preach the message that we have the "right" to healing or that we can "demand" a miracle? I find the thought of demanding anything from a king a disaster just waiting to happen. The Scriptures do declare that we can approach the throne of grace boldly, but please understand, the Bible is talking about how our mind-set should be toward God and how He understands our situations and is aware of how we feel. We can be confident that God cares and knows exactly what we are going through. But this boldness is not to be confused with a fool busting through the doors of the palace calling on the king in a loud voice, "Lord, You promised me healing...I demand a miracle!" I can just see a gleaming guillotine coming down on that rude intruder.

While God is not going to kill people for being inappropriate in His presence, why would the King listen to or give any regard to that intercessor? God doesn't *have* to do *anything*, and He is not subject to any party rules or regulations. There is no government that we can control in God's kingdom; our government is upon Christ's shoulders!

The anointing flows in and through the government of the kingdom of God. The governmental order of a theocracy is God first, then His King, and afterward everyone else. The sooner we accept the structure of heaven's government, the simpler the process will be of obtaining the anointing God has for His people. God is our Father, the King is Jesus, God's presence and power on earth is the Holy Spirit, and we are the meager serfs of His lands. He does not treat us as our insignificance would dictate, however; God calls us sons and daughters, Jesus calls us brothers and sisters, and the Holy Spirit calls us vessels and not vassals. To receive the anointing of the King, we must serve the King! The anointing flows down...

> Behold, how good and how pleasant it is
> for brethren to dwell together in unity! It is
> like the precious oil upon the head, running
> down on the beard, the beard of Aaron, run-
> ning down on the edge of his garments. It is
> like the dew of Hermon, descending upon the
> mountains of Zion; for there the LORD com-
> manded the blessing—life forevermore.
>
> —PSALM 133

...down from the Father...down to His people. But there is something to take notice of here in this passage of the Bible. The anointing flows in unity. This unity is the obedience to serve the Lord within the confines of His rulership as our King! The oil of this anointing described in the Psalms is that it flows down the head, down the beard, and upon the garments. The head of the church in God's realm is Jesus, our King. The anointing will flow from the Shepherd down upon the wisdom (beards represent elders and wisdom) of Christ's Word upon His garments (the people).

The kings of old have some of the most amazing robes. They would sew the flags and representations of all their conquered lands and other kings into the trains of their robes. Everyone would then see that this king was a conquering hero and bow before the king of nations. Our King's robe is so great, the train of His robe fills the whole temple. (The kingdoms of this world are the king-doms of our God and of His Son, the Christ.) That robe represents the devoted vessels that have become sub-missive to the King's rule. We align ourselves to receive

His holy anointing by serving the desires of our King. But there seems to be one thing that can and will break our connection to the King for this great impartation: disunity.

We may imagine unity as getting along and being somewhat amicable to each other. Unity is much more than that. Unity does not always allow individual expression, nor does it normally permit personal interdiction. Unity is the melding of hearts, minds, and actions of many for the benefit of all.

> Unity: the quality or state of not being multiple: oneness; a condition of harmony: accord; continuity without deviation or change (as in purpose or action)[1]

Unity is hard to attain and maintain without submission. But to whom are we to submit? Our friends? Our coworkers? Our employers? Our enemies? Yes to all of the above, but let's also add our *spiritual authority*.

There is an alarming trend that it creasing the fabric of our humanity worldwide: an utter lack of respect of and submission to authority. From our irreverent television shows, comedy sketches, and political pundits, the slippery slope of disrespect has been allowed to fester in our hearts. We have discovered a society that finds humor in debasing those who have any form of control or leadership in our existence. It seems that if a particular leader says or does something that we do not approve of, we are then obligated to bring him or her down with a maelstrom of cutting remarks and disapproving jest.

The church has allowed this to continue with, at best, silence and, at worst, reinforcing encouragement. This broad irreverence and dishonor have even become a narrative in the church. Members of the church body can be witnessed coming to church to sample the pastor's teaching like it was a fine wine and spitting out vehement denouncement if the vintage was not up to our liking or we felt the presentation was too cheap and easy. The empowerment of the believer is lost when we walk in disunity with our leadership, whether it is that of our government or our church.

The oil flows from the head of the church upon the beard of God's priest. Aaron was the high priest, and he carried the mantle of God's purity and word. He was the mouthpiece for God to the people. Jesus is our Good Shepherd, and He has given His church many under-shepherds (ministers and elders) who can help carry His Word to the people. This is the structure of God's government. When we try to diminish the importance of this leadership and order, we break the link to that holy anointing of heaven. We then find ourselves running to and fro, looking to absorb any wind of doctrine that will comfort us in our rebellion and soothe our troubled hearts that are full of misplaced loyalty. When we place ourselves in submission to our spiritual authority, the anointing flows as readily as a stream.

Be the Bride

When you read the Bible, how do you picture yourself? I used to picture myself as one of David's mighty men, a great judge over Israel like Samson, a prophet like Elisha, or even a disciple like Simon Peter. But as I've studied the Word of God more, I have adjusted my vision and perceptions. The New Testament brings clarity to our understanding of our identity in the kingdom of God. With regard to the kingdom Jesus is the King, and we are His future queen! Why is that a divine revelation to me? Because I'm a man...a man! Whenever I would read anything that pointed to the thought that I am regarded by Jesus as His bride, I would let out a slight *"yuck"* or *"c'mon, really?"* and continue with my reading. It is difficult for me to visualize myself as the "bride of Christ." I'm six-foot-three and over two hundred pounds of pure, powerful, handsome *man!* (Thank you for letting me share a little bit there...I'm also anointed! Ha!) How could I possibly be regarded as a "bride"? The very thought is confusing and repulsive to my masculinity. However, *compared to Jesus*—the One who spoke the world into existence, the One who created mountains and ecosystems with the words "Let there be...", the One who became a man and lived without sin, the One who died and then rose again from the dead—compared to Him, *I am* a bride! I'm not only a bride, as big and powerful as I may be as a man, I'm a prepubescent girl to Him! Jesus is Almighty God; we *are* His chosen bride.

Read the Scriptures from the perspective of a bride-to-be, and take your cues from other successful brides. A unique aspect of the lifestyle of a bride of Christ is how she responds to her groom. Study the brides who made their grooms proud. Nearly every woman in the Bible who has an encounter with Jesus Christ, the preincarnate Savior, or a type (foreshadowing example) of Jesus has that encounter at His feet. It is quite remarkable to read that these brides were submissive to the point of foot service, not merely lip service.

The Shunammite woman

This prominent woman had been cooking meals for the prophet Elisha for some time when God finally blessed her with a male child. Elisha had prophesied it in response to the Shunammite woman's incredible hospitality. When her son mysteriously died, the woman set off on a long journey to find the prophet. When she arrived at Mount Carmel, she grabbed hold of Elisha's feet and declared: "Did I ask a son of my Lord? Did I not say, 'Do not deceive me'?" (2 Kings 4:28). She further declared, "As the LORD lives, and as your soul lives, I will not leave you" (v. 30). She refused to give up on God, no matter if her dream of having a son was fulfilled or dashed upon the rocks of death. Broken devotion.

Ruth

Ruth was a young widow who committed herself to remain in covenant relationship with her mother-in-law even after her husband died unexpectedly. At the behest of her mother-in-law Ruth presented herself to a distant relative for redemption. If this kinsman decided to marry Ruth, her family would be saved from poverty and possible starvation. In a sincere act of obedience to Naomi, Ruth went out to Boaz during the night and lay down on the ground by his feet as he slept. Startled by this act of humility, Boaz asked what she wanted, and Ruth requested his redemption and protection. When Boaz accepted this gesture of surrender, Ruth and her family were saved, and the lineage of Christ received a new matriarch...Ruth!

Queen Esther

The Israelites were once again facing annihilation from their enemies, and only King Ahasuerus could grant mercy. Queen Esther had to risk her life in order to save the Israelites from complete slaughter. Under the leadership of her cousin Mordecai, Esther presented herself before the king and bowed at his feet. If King Ahasuerus rejected her uninvited visit to his throne room, she would be executed. Esther fasted and prayed and then proceeded to enter the king's presence. To Esther's relief and the salvation of Israel the king extended his scepter of permission to Esther, and when she touched it, the lives of all the Jews were preserved.

The Syrophoenician woman

This woman had crazy faith! Her daughter stricken with demon possession and needing a miracle, the Syrophoenician woman pleaded with Jesus to bring healing to her child. Jesus told her that He was called to the Jews of Israel and it wouldn't be good to take the food that was for His children and give it to the *little dogs*. Can you imagine Jesus calling someone a dog? That was one of the most insulting things you could ever call a person in that culture. Jesus was making a powerful distinction between the children of Israel and the Gentiles and Greeks who had infiltrated those holy lands. But the Syrophoenician woman was not put off by this statement. She replied, "Yes, Lord, yet even the little dogs eat the crumbs which fall from their masters' table" (Matt. 15:27). Jesus was amazed at her great faith and immediately spoke healing over her daughter. From that moment forward the people began bringing their sick and wounded to Jesus, and they laid them at His feet.

The bleeding woman

This woman had been bleeding for twelve years. The Bible never tells us what kind of bleeding problem she had contracted. She had been under the care of many doctors for it, and she had spent all her money, but instead of getting better, she grew worse. She heard about Jesus, and when He was coming by, she crawled up behind Him in the crowd and touched the tassel that hung down from His prayer shawl. She believed that if she could touch that tassel, she would be miraculously healed. Instantly when she touched it, she felt healing flow throughout her body. Jesus felt it too and asked who had touched Him. Eventually she came forward and told Him all she had believed for and received. Jesus blessed her and said, "Daughter, your faith has

healed you. Go in peace and be freed from your suffering" (Mark 5:34, NIV).

Mary

My favorite bride in the Bible is Mary. The motto of
her life seems to be "at His feet." Almost every time we
find this woman around the Christ, she was sitting or
serving at His feet.

Jesus was invited to a Pharisee's house for dinner,
and soon all the disciples were seated and ready to
dine. Mary came into the room and stood at the feet
of Christ as He was reclining at the table. She began to
weep, and her cries were so passionate that her tears fell
upon the feet of Christ. Mary quickly saw that her tears
were wetting the feet of her Master, and so she began to
wipe them dry with the hair from her head. Finally she
poured fragrant oil upon His feet to anoint them and
kissed His feet repeatedly in pure love and adoration.
This was not a normal or a casual scene in the time of
Christ. What Mary was doing was unheard of in Jewish
custom or society. It was not considered "couth" for a
Jewish person or even a Jewish slave to wash the feet of
their guests. The Jewish elite would usually reserve that
task for the Gentile slaves or the least prominent of all
the household servants. Mary had positioned herself at
the location where the household slaves would normally
stand (at the heels of the guests' feet). She was taking on
the role of a servant while she was yet quite the wealthy
and influential woman in the community. Jesus forgave

her sin and established her among the disciples along with her sister, Martha.

Not long after Mary's dramatic conversion, we find Jesus in another home, teaching and sharing with His disciples. Where was Mary? Sitting at His feet. Martha grew annoyed with Mary's lack of participation in the kitchen and household chores, and she came to Jesus looking for justice. Jesus told her that she was the one who was being distracted and making the mistake, stating that Mary had chosen the one thing that was needed...intimacy with Jesus.

When Jesus was delayed in coming to see this family, the brother of Mary and Martha, Lazarus, fell ill and died. They had sent word to Christ to come and heal him, but Jesus did not make it in time for Lazarus. He had been dead four days when Jesus finally arrived on the scene. Martha ran out to see Christ and proclaimed, "If You would have been here, Jesus, my brother wouldn't have died!" Jesus reminded Martha of His identity and His ability, and she reaffirmed her commitment and faith. When Mary came to Jesus, she fell down at His feet and had the same questions as Martha, but she received a different response and result: Jesus asked them to take Him to the graveside, and there He began to weep. Mary was not questioned about her faith, nor did she need a revelation; Mary knew Christ because she was the one who spent her time at His feet. Jesus raised Lazarus up from the dead and showed all the mourners there that He truly was the One sent from God.

Receiving all that God has for you is mostly a matter of position. For you to remember your place in God's kingdom brings glory to God in all that you do. We must humble ourselves and find ourselves at Jesus's feet. Each one of these brides demonstrates what it means to be broken and surrendered.

Scripture reads: "Humble yourselves under the mighty hand of God, and in his good time he will lift you up" (1 Pet. 5:6, TLB). Part of what it takes to bring ourselves to a place of humility is a feeble human understanding of the greatness and wonderment of God. Have you ever pondered the awesomeness of our Creator? You might think that I am selling you on the idea of mere meditation, but I am asking much more of you. We should be fanatical fans of all things God. Celebrate the Lord in all the things He does. All that He is and has made is for you! Devote time to thinking on the things that are described in Scripture that are excellent:

> Finally, brethren, *whatever* things are true, *whatever* things are noble, *whatever* things are just, *whatever* things are pure, *whatever* things are lovely, *whatever* things are of good report, if there *is* any virtue and if there *is* anything praiseworthy—meditate on these things.
> —PHILIPPIANS 4:8,
> EMPHASIS ADDED

Jesus is drawn to the praise of His people, and He cannot resist their affections. This anointing is not accomplished through ritual; it is received in a relationship that goes far beyond being "good." God wants us to be wholly owned, gladly and cheerfully. How happy would you be with your spouse if he or she told you every day how hard it was to be married to you? You probably wouldn't lavish as much blessing on them as you would on one who spoke to you with celebration regarding your actions and character. We must remember our place. That place is where the oil flows...down.

Mary kept herself in that place and received the blessings of a divine relationship. When Jesus was arrested in the Garden of Gethsemene, as they grabbed Him to take Him away, He spoke like a king. They asked if He was Jesus of Nazareth. When Jesus replied, "I am He," the Word tells us they all fell back to the ground! (See John 18:6.) Jesus had the power and authority in His speech like that of a king. But upon His arrest Jesus also smelled like a king, thanks to Mary.

While Jesus was being arraigned in a Jewish court, He told them of His throne. He told them He would be sitting at the right hand of the Father God and riding down upon the clouds. The Jews couldn't handle this revelatory truth and deemed it heresy and blasphemy. They began to spit on Him and beat Him, but Jesus still smelled like a king, thanks to Mary.

Before Pilate, Jesus kept His silence and spoke not in His own defense. Pilate marveled at His self-control and regal stature. Jesus stood there in silent submission, and He looked like a beat-up prisoner, but a slight breeze was blowing toward the governor's seat, and he picked up the aroma of a king, because of Mary.

Jesus was then brought before Herod. Herod couldn't get Jesus to do any miracles or signs for Him, and in disgust He placed a gorgeous robe on Him to mock His kingdom. Of course He was given a robe; even Herod couldn't deny that Jesus smelled like a king, all because of Mary.

When Jesus was beaten, nailed to the cross, crucified, pierced, and buried...He still smelled like a king, all because of Mary.

While many were being crucified, it was common for people to come by and vomit and urinate on the condemned person's feet. But when someone walked up to Jesus to oblige this culture of shame, they caught a whiff of the scent of a king, so lovingly caressed into the skin of Jesus's feet by whom? Mary.

And to whom did Jesus appear first, when He arose from the dead on the third day? Jesus appeared first to the one who had provided His anointing. The one who had placed herself in line and underneath her Savior. The one who had submitted herself as the bride and servant of the One who died for all mankind. Jesus appeared to Mary.

It is rather interesting that Mary did not recognize Jesus immediately when she met Him. Maybe in her grief her weeping had swollen her eyes, and they were hazed over with tears. Maybe it was because in her frantic desperation to look for Jesus's missing body, she wasn't even facing this supposed gardener. But when

Jesus answered her request for the location of Christ, He simply said, "Mary." I believe that she turned to look at the risen Savior, took a deep breath of the smell of His anointing, and said, "'Rabboni!' (which is to say, Teacher)" (John 20:16). The aroma of the anointing is an identifiable characteristic to the King and all those who submit themselves to Him. What do you smell like?

PART 3

THE RESULT:
VICTORIOUS LIVING

I AM SO EXCITED THAT YOU HAVE CONTINUED TO read and are willing to take all the steps necessary for your life to take a dramatic turn toward victory! This is the life of true freedom and success. This is an extraordinary life that is fulfilling and exciting. The things that are important to this lifestyle remain valuable, and those that have no eternal value fall away. The good news is that you will never miss them. The victory is not only in how you live for yourself but also in the impact you will have on the world around you. Welcome to life after death!

CHAPTER 9

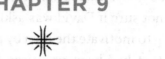

ROYAL REVELATIONS—
THE REWARDS OF THE KING

L ET'S GO BACK TO THE VALLEY OF ELAH AND witness how the shepherd boy responded to the champion of Gath. As Goliath came out to shout his usual diatribe toward the ranks of Israel, the Israeli soldiers began to lose heart. The men of Israel started running away when they saw Goliath. While they may have thought they were running *for* their lives, they were actually running *away* from victory in their lives.

David saw these men running and started to ask, "What shall be done for the man who kills this Philistine and takes away the reproach from Israel? For who is this uncircumcised Philistine, that he should defy the armies of the living God?" (1 Sam. 17:26).

The men told David, "Have you seen this man who has come up? Surely he has come to defy Israel; and it

139

shall be that man who kills him the king will enrich with great riches, will give him his daughter, and give his father's house exemption from taxes in Israel" (v. 25).

I am not sure if David was asking for himself or if he was trying to motivate the men by reminding them of the treasure that had been promised by the king. This was quite a significant offering to the man who would step up to this champion and go for the gold. The promise of the king of Israel was quite a gift and would raise the winning warrior to a status only second to that of the king himself. Can you see the correlation? God wants you to fight your champion and defeat it. And when you defeat your champion, God is promising a reward that no one can match.

I am so glad we serve a God who loves us and knows what it takes to motivate us. Jesus understands us and encourages us to help us succeed. Here's a key fact about the Lord: *God does not expect us to live for Him for free!* If you choose to kill the sin champion that is stifling your walk with Christ, the King of kings will hook you up even more than King Saul could ever bless David.

I've heard it said by many preachers that "PMS" has brought a great many leaders down! While we all chuckle at this not so subtle way of saying women have a lot of influence and power in the lives of men...this is exactly what King Saul offered the victor of this battle: power, money, and sex.

Royal Wealth

The first thing King Saul offered was to enrich the warrior who brought down the champion Goliath with great wealth. In the time of Saul there could be no one wealthier than the king. The king received his wealth by taking a portion of all the people's proceeds. Royalty has wealth that no one else can claim...generational wealth as well as continual income from the increase of the people who paid their taxes to the crown. If you do not live in a land with a governmental monarchy, it is hard to understand the tremendous differences between royal wealth and common riches. Common riches are no less financially impacting in a person's life, but it is a different kind of fiscal consideration that is given to royalty. Royal wealth is quite a different story when it comes to day-to-day living.

The queen of England employs my wife's cousin. She maintains the accounting for the payroll of all the queen's palaces and facilities. This is a prestigious position, and I marvel at her access to so much history and honored traditions. I can only imagine what it would be like to have an audience with the queen. That would be a wonderful moment for me, and I would cherish it most eagerly. I earnestly hope that I would once be able to go to a royal function and be counted as one of those who were in the presence of actual royalty.

On a different note, Bill Gates walks into a McDonald's...This is not the start of a Bill Gates joke; this is the scene we are going to discover. Bill arrives at the counter of this restaurant and makes his lunch request. "I'll have a Big Mac and french fries with a Diet Coke." The man behind the counter smiles at him and says, "Aren't you Bill Gates?" Bill nods his head and smiles slightly as the man says, "Dude, I can't believe Bill Gates is in my McDonald's. This is crazy!" The restaurant manager never cracks a smile, but he declares, "I'm an Apple guy myself! Too many stinking viruses in those PCs!" They hand Bill Gates his food order, and Bill takes a black American Express card out of his billfold to pay for his meal. Bill has more than enough money to pay for this meal; he could actually buy the entire McDonald's corporation with his checkbook and make sure that manager never works in another of his newly acquired locations ever again. Did you know that Bill Gates pays millions of dollars a day in tax penalties for the current formulation of his companies, and he pays it willingly because changing the way Microsoft and Intel do things would cost him more per day than the several millions he pays to the government? That is common riches. Someone with riches has the money to buy whatever he wants whenever he wants.

But when the queen of England walks into a McDonald's, it is a completely different story. First of all, whenever the queen plans to go somewhere, there must be a plan in place. She cannot go to places that are unable to receive her entourage and guard. She cannot visit places that have not been prepared for her. When she enters the restaurant, there is a celebration and a proclamation: "Ladies and gentlemen, the queen of England!" People begin to clap and whistle. People lift their kids over their heads so that they can catch a glimpse of this woman of royal distinction. Trumpets sound and the Yeomen of the Guard stand at attention with their lances at the ready. The queen, while diminutive in stature, walks the center of the red carpet and waves at her subjects who are enjoying their cheeseburgers and fries with much joy. As the queen approaches the ordering counter, the manager is beside himself with glee and can be seen curtsying to the queen even though he is a male. The raucous din is finally abated when the queen raises a hand for silence. All in attendance are fixated on her every word, wondering what delicacy brought their sovereign to such a common place for dining fare. The queen regally states, "I believe I would like a McRoyale with cheese, chips, and an iced tea, please." The manager flies from the counter after yet another inappropriate curtsy and a "Yes, ma'am. Right away, ma'am!" The fawning manager is quickly replaced by the smoother-talking owner, who returns in mere seconds with the queen's order as such: "Ma'am, here is your order. I would like you to know that I picked those tomatoes fresh from my garden, I hand-selected your lettuce, we killed the fatted calf for your burger meat, and I licked and stuck each and every sesame on your hamburger bun! We did it all for you!" The owner bows low to the ground as only a theatrical maven would do, as the queen replies with sincerity and kindness, "Henry, would you please pay this gentleman?" Now what do you think the McDonald's owner would say to the queen that he didn't say to Bill Gates? He would reply,

"No, ma'am, please take this meal with our compliments. Thank you for coming to visit us here at McDonald's. It has been a pleasure for us to share our products and service with you!"

Did you catch that? Royalty receives privileges and honor that commoners do not. Royals are quite wealthy, but in no way are they the richest people in the world. What is unique about royal wealth is that is goes far beyond bank accounts and investment portfolios. Royal wealth means that you have the money to buy the things that you want and need, but you don't always have to. Royal wealth is receiving the blessings of the things you want that cannot be bought with riches. The royals of Europe were often described as "blue bloods." These were people of noble birth or from a prominent family within government and society. They were wealthy enough to pay common people to go out and labor for them in the fields. Because of their lack of sun and weather exposure, their skin was translucent and pale. The royals' blue veins therefore stood out quite dramatically, and they were called "blue bloods." Because of their prominence, they rarely died as young as their laborers and subjects. It was believed that these people had God's blessing on their lives and that long life was afforded them from God.

The Lord wants to bless you with royal wealth. Common riches are nice, but money can't solve all the issues that we face on a continual basis. You can't buy long life, but God promises us a long, fulfilling life if we honor our mothers and fathers:

> Honor your father and your mother, that your
> days may be long upon the land which the
> LORD your God is giving you.
> —EXODUS 20:12

You can't buy physical health, but God promises us
an abundant life if we keep Him as the center and focus
of our lives:

> The thief does not come except to steal, and
> to kill, and to destroy. I have come that they
> may have life, and that they may have it more
> abundantly.
> —JOHN 10:10

You can't buy salvation and deliverance for your children and grandchildren, but God says that He will bless
thousands of generations of those who love Him and
keep His commandments:

> For I, the LORD your God, am a jealous God,
> visiting the iniquity of the fathers upon the
> children to the third and fourth generations
> of those who hate Me, but showing mercy to
> thousands, to those who love Me and keep My
> commandments.
> —EXODUS 20:5–6

Royal wealth is wonderful for the things money can't
buy. True security cannot be installed like an alarm
system. Our protection comes from the Lord. Peace in
your heart and mind is not available in a pill or a potion.
Peace must be received from its Prince, Jesus:

For unto us a Child is born, unto us a Son is given; and the government will be upon His shoulder. And His name will be called Wonderful, Counselor, Mighty God, Everlasting Father, *Prince of Peace.*

—ISAIAH 9:6,
EMPHASIS ADDED

Be anxious for nothing, but in everything by prayer and supplication, with thanksgiving, let your requests be made known to God; and the peace of God, which surpasses all understanding, will guard your hearts and minds through Christ Jesus.

—PHILIPPIANS 4:6–7

God will also grant us joy! Joy cannot be stopped or even hindered by situations and emotions. Joy is the abundance of God's blessing that is bestowed upon all that He loves and all who love Him.

All the royal wealth will be bestowed upon the person who kills their champion and decides to live a life of victory. God's wealth is laid up for you; all you have to do it defeat sin to take hold of it.

Royal Relationships

Living in victory includes the blessing of royal relationships. King Saul promised that the killer of Goliath would receive his daughter's hand in marriage. While we might pause to reflect on how sad a day that could possibly be for Saul's daughter Michal, it was an amazing opportunity for the victor. What would happen if the greatest fighter in all the land were also the ugliest man in the land? What if he had warts, five eyes, bad breath, and smelled like camel droppings? I guess she would have to deal with it, but wow, that would be a nightmare!

The daughters of kings throughout history were charged to marry for principles bigger than themselves. The children of kings and queens usually married for the kingdom and not for love. Their royal weddings were arranged marriages. These unions usually linked countries and government leaders to provide lasting peace and safety to a kingdom or region. These marriages protected, provided for, and grew the kingdom and were vital to the success of a king's reign. The kids of the king understood their role in history. Even as luxury and excess were at their fingertips, the looming thought of kingdom obligations overshadowed them. They must live in a way that upholds the kingdom, and their relationships must also promote the same.

I believe in arranged marriages today. Now before you throw this book into the fireplace and say I've lost my mind, hear me out. Our salvation—wait, *our lives*—were purchased by Jesus when He died on the cross. How much freedom do we have in this area? A great many marriages fail today because they have no purpose and no meaning. We should marry for something that is greater than us. We should be marrying for the benefit of the kingdom. When it comes to selecting the person with whom you will spend the rest of your life, it is important to be deliberate. Use the kingdom as a measuring stick. How will you better the kingdom of God by marrying this person? Will marriage to this person add to the godliness and effectiveness of your life for God? Do you do things for God together, or is all your time wasted in selfish, fleshly pursuits? Are you planning to bear world-changing children, or do you only want your kids to be happy and healthy? Will you do more for God's kingdom together than you could possibly do apart? That is the question!

The thought of marrying whomever your parents decide for you to marry may seem foreign to many people. But single Christians are crouching at the door of rebellion at any form of parental intervention when it comes to a future mate. And yet they will go online and allow Internet dating sites, social media relationship tests, telephone psychics, and even astrological charts tell them whom they can date. These people will listen to a computer program, a hacker, or a demon-possessed liar tell them whom to marry, but they won't trust someone who loves them? They will even listen to friends and neighbors give them advice, but their rebellion has gotten so intense that they don't want to bring that potential mate home to meet their parents!

There is more at stake in our relationships than upsetting our potential spouses with negativity from our family. That individual is attempting to join your family, and conversely you are joining theirs.

There's much more to royal relationships than arranged marriages, although I know I had you reading earnestly when I addressed it. Royal relationships are built on the premise of "whatever it takes for the kingdom." This ideal is important for the longevity of and commitment to the relationship. Have you ever noticed that royals do not often divorce? During a time when we are experiencing nearly half of Christians marriages worldwide ending in divorce, something must be said. The standard statement in a divorce court as the reason for separation is "irreconcilable differences." In other words, the couple feels there are too many problems in the relationship that they just cannot be solved. Royals do not often divorce, because they don't marry so that all their problems will go away. Royals marry to solve major problems together. That significant other in your life is not there to solve all of your problems; you are to serve each other and love each other as you together reach out to others.

The preparation for a lasting relationship is supposed to begin long before you even consider dating or marriage. The Bible says that there is a great miracle that takes place in marriage: two become one flesh. That is an important mathematical equation, founded in a miraculous conclusion. Two whole numbers become one whole number: one plus one equals one. This equation requires that there be two whole, healthy, royal people to become one. You cannot have royal relationships when you marry a commoner. You should not be unequally yoked with an unbeliever in marriage. That just causes all kinds of problems, because your spouse won't understand your motivating desire to live for the kingdom. How can you possibly live with someone who finds the very core principles you've built your life upon to be unnecessary—or even worse, as lies? To be whole you have to be at a place in your life where you are spiritually, morally, socially, and mentally mature.

The royal relationships that God prescribes allow us to carry a new standard to the next generation. Did you come from a home with divorce, abuse, poverty, or addiction? God's blessings are following you and will overtake you as you claim the victory over that sin champion. Your children will not have to deal with these issues in their home as long as you evict the champion of sin from the battlefield of your mind, heart, and home. You are starting a new legacy among your offspring. This legacy will eclipse the past and all the failures that may have marred your childhood. Your kids will never know the sting of verbal abuse, the shame of addiction, or the pain of divorce. They will know a royal life, a peaceful life, a godly life.

People seem to enjoy a little drama in their lives: dramatic television shows, dramatic musical pieces, dramatic movies, dramatic sermons, even dramatic video games. While I don't mind an exciting bit of entertainment, I absolutely abhor relationship drama. It hurts my heart to hear about people who hurt each other or their kids with their words or deeds. I don't find that entertaining at all, and I usually will turn the channel or walk out of the theater because it bothers me. I know that my sensitivity is based upon my calling as a motivational speaker. I get to travel all over the world and speak to businesses and students about the power of positive choices. I talk to business professionals and students about loving people. Many times, at the end of my presentations, I hear tearful stories from both the students and the professionals. They share with me their stories of pain and suffering at the hands of people who said they cared about them. I cry with these people and share hope with them. Since I speak to hundreds of thousands every year around the globe, it is tough for me to sit in a theater or in front of a television and listen to people's stories of pain and laugh or be entertained by them. It is not entertaining to me; it's sad. I've even caught myself praying for fictional characters on certain programs that found themselves in troubling situations. I want to go up to them, hug them, and tell them they are going to be OK.

I have always wanted to have a boring relationship with my family. I want everyone to be fulfilled in their lives but unsatisfied with the status quo. I want all of our excitement to be found in pursuing great things for others and reaching out to people in love. Royal relationships endeavor to live as an example to the kingdom. No one looks at the royals and thinks about how many struggles they have. Consistency and patience are keys to that end. One of my greatest pleasures is coming home from a ministry or motivational assignment and greeting my family as I enter the door. My sons run up to me and hug me, screaming, "Daddy!" My wife is always a couple of steps behind them, saying, "Hey, honey! We missed you." Then she gives me a kiss (ahh, yes!). Then I ask a pertinent question, "How are things?"

and the most wonderful thing I can possibly hear is, "Everything's fine." Ahhhhh! Boring! That's like the elixir of joy to me! If you have a "boring" life, then you can be utilized to aid others, and you will not be caught up in a spiral of narcissism.

God wants us to kill sin. When sin is destroyed from our midst, there is a beautiful exchange from old hag (common spouse) to royal wife, or arrogant jerk (nominal mate) to royal husband. We inspire generations that follow us to live in the ways of the kingdom that they possess. We begin to strive for God's kingdom with the love and care the nations need so desperately. Where do we get the time and opportunities to accomplish world domination? We have so much more time to offer because we do these things with our family, not in spite of them. We spend less time fighting and more time loving and reaching out. A boring life can be yours if you kill the champion!

Royal Influence

The king promised that if any man killed the champion, he would also exempt that man's father's family (that means the entire family lineage) from taxes for life. Wow! I can say with all sincerity that I hate paying my taxes. I hate, hate, hate, hate, hate paying taxes. It's not that I don't appreciate all that my government does for me: the roads that it builds, schools, bridges, parks, museums, police, military, and the judicial system. I just hate giving up money out of my paycheck for anything.

I don't even enjoy shopping. It has been said that shopping is supposed to produce a measure of endorphins to the brain, but my brain only feels sorrow as the dollars fly into the cash register of the local store. So when I hear that I could go on with my life and not pay any taxes...I get excited!

When you kill sin and take dominion over your existence, you get the influence of the king. You still have to pay taxes to your government, so please do not misunderstand me. When the tax collectors show up at your workplace or home because you haven't been doing your duty, don't come crying to me. *I told you* to pay those taxes, people! But the influence of the king is more than exemption from taxes. It is the actual promise to achieve the status of royalty. Royalty has influence that no one else can attain. It has the attention of the people that are being led. Royal persons have responsibilities that require them to serve as ambassadors for the nation that they represent. Royals must live at a level that others would ascribe as great and glorious. They are not encumbered by the day-to-day mundane tasks of a common person. They must spend the majority of their time leading and motivating people to accomplish great things for the advancement of their society.

God wants to give you the status and influence of the kingdom. The only people who don't pay taxes to the crown are the king and the king's family. For King Saul to offer this as an incentive to kill the champion Goliath was quite an interesting turn of events. This would put

Israel's warring victor on the same level as the king when it came to tax status.

In many countries today the only people who do not pay taxes to the government are the president, kings, and dictators. I am not sure why these governments do not require the payment of taxes from their various supreme rulers. There is certainly a need for more government funding, and the leader has plenty of funds.

I do have a theory regarding supreme leaders and taxes that will possibly bring this teaching into clear focus. I believe that we allow our leadership to be exempt from taxes because we are making a specific declaration to their authorities: "President, king, or dictator, we do not want you to worry about paying taxes during your time and terms of service. We don't want you to spend hours of your time trying to figure out your tax returns or even paying others to do them for you. We don't want you to try to organize your finances and tax payments so they look better to us, or the governing finance authorities. What we need you to do is lead our country into victory and success: success in finances, success in education, success in justice, success in social reform, success in protection, and success in enterprise."

The Lord wants to give you the status of a king. He wants to endow you with the ability to be heard from heaven. God wants you to have authority in heaven and on earth. He will grant you the ability to pray anything in His name and receive an answer from His throne.

> Most assuredly, I say to you, he who believes
> in Me, the works that I do he will do also; and
> greater works than these he will do, because I
> go to My Father. And whatever you ask in My
> name, that I will do, that the Father may be
> glorified in the Son. If you ask anything in My
> name, I will do it.
>
> —JOHN 14:12–14

That is so amazing! The very thought that we can
come into the palace of the king in prayer and request
an audience, at any time we wish, and He responds with
favor upon us...priceless!

God cares about what His victors do with their time.
He doesn't want you spending your time on menial tasks
that have little eternal significance. He wants us to work
hard, but not be overly concerned about non-kingdom-
related needs.

> Therefore I say to you, do not worry about
> your life, what you will eat or what you will
> drink; nor about your body, what you will put
> on. Is not life more than food and the body
> more than clothing? Look at the birds of the
> air, for they neither sow nor reap nor gather
> into barns; yet your heavenly Father feeds
> them. Are you not of more value than they?
> Which of you by worrying can add one cubit
> to his stature?
>
> So why do you worry about clothing?
> Consider the lilies of the field, how they grow:
> they neither toil nor spin; and yet I say to

you that even Solomon in all his glory was not arrayed like one of these. Now if God so clothes the grass of the field, which today is, and tomorrow is thrown into the oven, will He not much more clothe you, O you of little faith? Therefore do not worry, saying, "What shall we eat?" or "What shall we drink?" or "What shall we wear?" For after all these things the Gentiles seek. For your heavenly Father knows that you need all these things. But seek first the kingdom of God and His righteousness, and all these things shall be added to you. Therefore do not worry about tomorrow, for tomorrow will worry about its own things. Sufficient for the day is its own trouble.

—MATTHEW 6:25–34

God cares about every single part of your existence, and He is focused on you having the best life possible. If He is concerned with that for you, you need not be overly self-consumed. Spend all your time building His kingdom. Spend every waking hour trying to reach people for Jesus, sharing your food, money, wisdom, time, talent, hope, excitement, testimony, tears, and laughter. I am sure there is a lot more that you can do on a continual basis to ensure that a victorious life is shared by the world. The status of the king requires that we avail ourselves to use our influence to make the world a better place through the power of Christ.

CHAPTER 10

CLEAN IT UP—
GUILT-FREE IS THE
WAY TO BE

THERE IS NO BETTER FEELING THAN TO BE free of guilt and regrets. I will never forget some of those all-night study sessions while I was a university student. I would cram and prepare and quiz myself to the point of exhaustion. The best feeling I would feel was not when I saw a good grade on the wall, but when I walked out of that exam and knew that I had done my best. I had effectively studied, prepared, and knew the lessons. My grades did not always reflect my knowledge of the subject and my grasp of the principles learned. But what I still apply to my life from that class is what's most valuable to me.

Whenever I bring up the term *holiness*, it seems people all begin to squirm in their seats and become super-defensive. We have all had people complain about something that we are doing and tell us that since it is not the gray area of life that they enjoy, it must be sin for us. Relax, my friend, that is not what I am here to address. You will be much better off if you concentrate on what has eternal significance instead of what you're doing that doesn't. Holiness involves a passionate love for God that leads to living without guilt and regret.

> There is therefore now no condemnation to those who are in Christ Jesus, who do not walk according to the flesh, but according to the Spirit. For the law of the Spirit of life in Christ Jesus has made me free from the law of sin and death.
> —ROMANS 8:1–2

After Jesus was anointed at Bethany by Mary, all hell broke loose in His life: Judas agreed to betray Him; He sweat blood in the Garden; He was arrested and abandoned by His disciples; false witnesses lied about Him to the court; Peter denied Him three times; He was beaten and mocked by Pilate, Herod, the Roman soldiers, the Jews, and a thief on the cross next to Him; He was crucified; and He died. Yet after all the things that Jesus endured to purchase our salvation, He regrets none of it!

> Then He said to them, "These are the words which I spoke to you while I was still with you, that all things must be fulfilled which were written in the Law of Moses and the Prophets and the Psalms concerning Me." And He

opened their understanding, that they might comprehend the Scriptures. Then He said to them, "Thus it is written, and thus it was necessary for the Christ to suffer and to rise from the dead the third day, and that repentance and remission of sins should be preached in His name to all nations, beginning at Jerusalem. And you are witnesses of these things. Behold, I send the Promise of My Father upon you; but tarry in the city of Jerusalem until you are endued with power from on high." And He led them out as far as Bethany, and He lifted up His hands and blessed them. Now it came to pass, while He blessed them, that He was parted from them and carried up into heaven. And they worshiped Him, and returned to Jerusalem with great joy, and were continually in the temple praising and blessing God.

—LUKE 24:44–53

Jesus doesn't sound resentful or angry, does He? No, the Lord Jesus understood what had to be done for our transformation, and He was willing to pay the ultimate price. He expects us to be willing to do the same. To lay down our lives for Jesus is much harder than dying for Jesus. Dying requires a lot less effort than waking up every day and doing what it takes to share our faith and praise to God with our neighbors.

Choosing Relationships That Help You Live With No Regrets

Living pure before God and men is not easy, but it will lead to a life of no regrets. People will always tell you that you are wasting your life, just as the disciples told Mary that she wasted that anointing oil. I'd have to ask those people, "What am I missing?" I mean, really, what do I have to gain from a life of impurity? David was given King Saul's armor to go and fight Goliath, but he didn't use it.

> So Saul clothed David with his armor, and he put a bronze helmet on his head; he also clothed him with a coat of mail. David fastened his sword to his armor and tried to walk, for he had not tested them. And David said to Saul, "I cannot walk with these, for I have not tested them." So David took them off.
> —1 SAMUEL 17:38–39

Sometimes we allow the wrong people to be involved in the decision-making of our lives. We think that they are there to help us and be a positive influence in our lives, but time and experience show them for who and what they are. We must be willing to let some of these dead-end relationships dissolve if we expect to live in victory. I'm not talking about people whom you may not agree with on nonessential topics and issues. I'm speaking to relationships that are a constant source of discouragement from the life of victory that you are pursuing.

Some of the best relationships in my life are with people who at one time or another disagreed with me about issues or situations. Some of them have had heated disagreements with me about things that we thought were important or valuable at the time. But by the end of the scenario, we would agree that what really mattered was our friendship, and we would remain in relationship and fellowship. Those are now my closest friends. We understand that nothing will separate us because we won't allow it.

David was unwilling to take an untested set of armor into battle. He was smart in being unwilling to do so, because in the heat of battle you need to be able to move free of hindrances and encumbrances that would keep you from acting.

The wrong relationships can restrain your freedom in the Lord and restrict your ability to reach other people. You don't want to take your Muslim acquaintance with you to share your faith with an unbeliever at work. You keep sharing Jesus with both, but you know that it's hard to move with that friend present, so you make sure they have a place in your life but not in your outreach. You don't know how they would react to your "proselytizing" in the marketplace, and it's not worth the distraction.

The same is true of holiness. As you are living a regret-free existence, you must put all of your relationships in the appropriate frame in your life. Are you reaching them? Are they reaching you? Are they following God? Are you better because of them? Are you worse because of them? Not everyone is fit for the journey you are taking. Living guilt-free involves making sure everyone you know and meet understands whom you serve by simply hearing and observing you. Living victorious is living in such a way that what you say and how you live points people to the logical conclusion: that you are a true believer.

CHAPTER 11

MENTALLY CHALLENGED

GOLIATH WASN'T THE ONLY PROBLEM DAVID had to face that day in the Valley of Elah. David's big brother Eliab walked up and started to accuse his younger brother of trying to stir up trouble and coming to see the battle just for its entertainment value. David was actually on an assignment from his father, Jesse, who had sent him to bring gifts to David's brothers and the commanding officer over them. Jesse had also asked David to bring back some of the spoils from the war. Little did Jesse know, the whole army was a bunch of scaredy-cat sissies, and no one had fought at all. Eliab is indicative of the place where you are right now in reading this book. Eliab could be described as a class-one "hater," especially after he was passed over by the prophet Samuel to be anointed as Israel's next king.

God told Samuel:

Do not look at his appearance or his physical
stature, because I have refused him. For the
LORD does not see as man sees; for man looks
at the outward appearance, but the LORD
looks at the heart.

—1 SAMUEL 16:7–8

God did not choose Eliab: the tall and stately one.
God did not choose Abinadab: the royal and regal one.
Neither did God choose Shammah: the famous and tal-
ented one. God chose the *least* of the brothers for His
great task. What stature, talent, ability, and nobility
cannot do, God can do in *you*!

Chosen for a Cause

The enemy, or even your own family, might be telling
you that this book is not that important and that you
need to go do something else right now. While you may
need to be obedient to pertinent things, do not let the
enemy distract you from the journey of transformation
that lies within these pages. Do not be distracted by an
irritated wife, husband, or family member and allow
your moment to be lost in another argument. God has
chosen you for this moment to be the one who walks
in victory. Be patient, as David was. David said, "What
have I done now? Is there not a cause?" (1 Sam. 17:29).
There *is* a cause here; keep the goal of your pursuit of
God's best for your life in mind. Don't get trapped in the
mire of things around you that wish to derail this transformation in your life.

Our cause is the advancement of the kingdom of God. The kingdom must first possess us, then the world around us. People may disagree with our cause. They may feel that what you and I are spending our time on is a reckless pursuit of spirituality. I disagree. This is a responsible pursuit of victory. There will be times when you will feel as if you have to defend your lifestyle to your friends and family. Understand that in the game of victorious life in the spirit there are winners and there are losers.

This Game Can't Be Taken Lightly

I have learned a great many things about people and life from sporting events. I am constantly amazed at the rabidity of the sports fan. World Cup fans will dress up in costumes, paint their faces and bodies, shout, chant, and sing for their teams. When their team is winning, they will sing for joy, and when their team is losing, they will shout encouragement. They even come up with super-annoying instruments, such as the vuvuzela, that drive players mad while on the pitch. This is all in good fun and sport, but there can be a dark side to the rabid sports fan.

There is a species of sports fan that likes to deride the other team more than they like cheering for their favorite team. These fans can be heard saying the most cruel and obnoxious things and will even cheer when an opposing player is injured during the match. These are not the best of fans, and many athletes complain about the antics of these fools.

You are in the game of your life. You are willing to kill the champion of sin and are getting ready to go out and face the challenge. Meanwhile, some rabid fan of sin is telling you to abort your mission of excellence and purity. They invite you to go to that nightclub and hang out. The rabid fan of sin in your life may be a boyfriend or girlfriend who feels it is only normal that you live together before marriage and engage in premarital sexual activity. There is an endless stream of scenarios in which these fans will shout out complaints and godless arguments to knock you off your game. I know that your coach says not to listen to them, and he is right. You don't have to listen to what they are saying, but you're not deaf, so how do you respond to what you're hearing?

Respond with the words of David: "Is there not a cause?" Remind yourself that the battle you are fighting and the game you are playing is not for a trophy or an award. You are in a battle for your soul. This is a game for eternity, and it cannot be taken lightly. Think about this temptation and how it will affect your eternity. Would you be willing to sacrifice your divine relationship, which will last for eternity, for a temporal pleasure that will last only minutes? How willing are you to fail your eternal husband for an ungodly girlfriend or boyfriend? How will this action affect all those with whom you have so eagerly shared your faith? Is there not a cause? We cannot let the enemy jeer us off the pitch.

The devil is losing, and he will say anything and everything to try to get us to fail. Why entertain the losing side when you're winning? What if this were the last day you got this chance to live for the Lord—how would it be to face Him immediately after this moment? Don't let the loser of hell call *you* a loser...you are more than a conqueror in Jesus Christ!

Wisdom From the Word Will Help You Win!

I find that many more mental games originate in my own heart. The biggest hater of my victorious destiny is the sin nature inside me. I have talked myself out of more victories than any demon ever could. We must take the Word of God and apply it to the problem. When you and I read the Bible, we are allowing ourselves to be changed and washed...brainwashed...as if we have used a bottle of detergent on our minds. The Word will help us overcome the vain thoughts and sinful imaginations that desire to control us and distract us from the battlefield.

> For the weapons of our warfare are not carnal
> but mighty in God for pulling down strong-
> holds, casting down arguments and every high
> thing that exalts itself against the knowledge
> of God, bringing every thought into captivity
> to the obedience of Christ, and being ready to
> punish all disobedience when your obedience
> is fulfilled.
> —2 CORINTHIANS 10:4–6

One of the biggest mind games the enemy wants to put in your way is your ability to read and understand the Word of God. I used to struggle reading the Bible in a diabolical way. When I was a teenager, I remember the Bible being a book that I would read out of obligation and guilt. I would almost always fall asleep while reading it, and I remember times reading the Book of Numbers to actually help me fall asleep! One day I grew frustrated with my growing apathy about the Word of God, and I decided to do something about it. I prayed and asked God for help: "Lord, I don't want to make You mad or anything...but I really hate reading the Bible. It's not fun, and I feel like I'm not getting anything out of it! I like movies, Jesus! I would watch the Bible in a movie all day long and not ever fall asleep or get bored. If You could somehow make the Bible into a movie in my mind, God, it would really help. Amen." I had no idea what I was doing, but God answered that fifteen-year-old's prayer. He gave me insight and revelation from the Scriptures that made the Bible come alive to me, and it truly is like a movie screen in my mind. My preaching and motivational speaking is fundamentally based on my grasp of the Bible. Often people mention that while I speak they can see the story in their minds; I attribute 100 percent of that revelation to God's wisdom.

There are a few times in the Bible where the Lord allows us to ask for certain things that we will automatically receive. Wisdom is one of those things.

> But let patience have its perfect work, that
> you may be perfect and complete, lacking
> nothing. If any of you lacks wisdom, let him
> ask of God, who gives to all liberally and
> without reproach, and it will be given to him.
> But let him ask in faith, with no doubting, for
> he who doubts is like a wave of the sea driven
> and tossed by the wind.
>
> —JAMES 1:4–6

When Solomon asked the Lord for wisdom, God
was so pleased that He gave Solomon wealth, long life,
and peace on every side from his enemies. Wisdom is
a gateway to the good life in Christ. Ask for wisdom
daily, and see what God does in and through you! When
I asked God to help me read the Bible and understand
and digest it properly, I was asking Him for divine
wisdom. God is wisdom, so when you ask Him for that,
you are asking Him for more of Himself in you! That's
a sure way to become God's favorite…I know I am!
(Technically, all of us are, but who's keeping track?)

CHAPTER 12

GOAL!—MY FAVORITE PART
OF SOCCER/FOOTBALL!

I WAS IN THE KITCHEN GRABBING MY LUNCH BEFORE I left for school. I had all my favorites that day: peanut butter and marshmallow fluff sandwich, potato chips, baby carrots, celery and peanut butter, a Snickers candy bar, a banana, and a juice box. I was meditating on how great this lunch was going to be when my mom interrupted my peaceful thought process with a brain-busting, Confucius-like moral: "Allen, today you need to do things that will matter five minutes after the Rapture takes place." I honestly had no idea what this wise woman of power (that's for you, Mommy!) was talking about, but I never forgot what she said. Later I reflected on her words, and it struck me in a unique fashion. What will matter five minutes after we are all in heaven?

When we all get to heaven, there will be television shows broadcast throughout glory. There will be sporting events with perfect scores, quiz shows with perfect results, and talk shows with perfect guests. The most popular talk show will be the apostle Peter's show called *Rock Talk*. *Rock Talk* has the highest praise ratings in heaven because it celebrates Jesus with powerful testimonies from history's most powerful Christ followers. You and I finally get enough glory days in our account to get entrance to a live production of the show.

The guests today are some of the greatest leaders in history. Simon Peter calls on his first guest, King Solomon! Solomon comes out in regal robes of righteousness and blessing, and as he shares his testimony, people are in awe. We all sit back in our seats and close our eyes; we just breathe in the wisdom of the ages as this powerful orator speaks about the height, depth, and greatness of God's love. Solomon's speaking is so amazing that nine hundred years slip by without even so much as a commercial break, as no one wants to interrupt this flow of wisdom and insight.

As soon as Solomon completes his stories of God's great love, we break for commercials. We hear yet another announcement about the newest flavors of manna available in the Café of Tranquility. Heavenly hash? We'll see!

The second guest on *Rock Talk* is none other than Solomon's father, King David! The crowd roars with joy as the psalmist enters the arena with a case filled with instruments. David leads a procession of worship hymns and spiritual songs. It is a great privilege to experience how these ancient choruses were originally performed, instead of the cheap imitations we have heard over the centuries. We sing the praises of God for what seems like ages (and it is), until David begins to write new songs for the Lord, right on the spot! Worship hasn't been this much fun since they threw that old devil into the bottomless pit!

The final guest of *Rock Talk* is an unschooled ordinary man. He comes out to much less fanfare and celebration. People are more interested in his experiences with Christ than the stories of all he's accomplished. His name is John. The one whom Jesus loved is standing center stage with a lone spotlight on his stocky form. His eyes are kind and his hands expressive as he tells his tales of Jesus. His stories about Jesus are as intricate and delicate as a lace garment... woven in truth and humility.

John is able to tell the audience at *Rock Talk* what it was like to live with and for Jesus. John never turned away when Jesus was arrested, John never denied Christ, John was standing at the foot of the cross when Jesus died, and he was there when He rose again! John tells of the Upper Room, where he spoke in tongues and was filled with power to do God's work. He even shares the emotion he felt upon hearing the lives of the other disciples had been laid upon the altars of world transformation.

John concludes his dialogue with a powerful sentiment: "Many people merely give their hearts to Jesus for a season; I was blessed to give my whole life to Him. Praise be to the only wise God, my Savior!"

As John walks away from center stage, Peter eyes the cameraman nervously and motions to keep the cameras rolling…the crowd immediately erupts into a spontaneous applause of praise to the Lord as Peter shouts, "I must share my story tonight!" You and I look at each other and shrug our shoulders as we settle into our seats for a bit of extra *Rock Talk*.

Peter shares that Solomon had a powerful discourse, David had an anointed song, and John shared an intimate portrait of Christ…but Simon Peter has a tragedy to share. Simon tells of how he was the most outspoken of the disciples, sharing his heart freely with Christ even though he sometimes was rebuked for thoughts contrary to Christ's will. But nothing compared to the time when Jesus told him that he would deny Him three times. Peter said it would never happen, but sure enough Peter found himself doing just that when the appointed hour arrived. Simon felt like such a failure and wanted to quit. What kept him going was what he'd learned from all his other mistakes: Jesus would forgive him. And forgive him He did, at the seashore days after rising from the dead.

Jesus asked Peter three times: "Do you love Me?" Peter tells us how he was hurt and embarrassed because he knew why Jesus asked him that question three times, but he was determined to live without failing Christ again. But what was this? Jesus said he was going to suffer and die for His sake…"No matter!" Peter said. "I will not deny my Savior ever again!"

Simon begins to praise the Lord for the triumphs that immediately followed Pentecost. After the filling of the Spirit, thousands were saved at one time. He spoke the Word of God boldly and turned the world upside down with his preaching. Even Gentiles were being converted and transformed by this gospel for all mankind. Peter shared that as he would walk about, his shadow would fall upon people and heal them. (Oh, what amazing fun we could have with *that* ability! Cue musical score: "Me and my shadow…healing people at the maall!") Peter said all seemed well, but there was a storm of persecution brewing.

Persecution scattered the saints and spread the gospel even farther around the world. That same persecution came looking for Peter. Peter tells about his wife's arrest and murder at the hands of cruel men, how he was unable to save her and she died for the gospel. Then it was Peter's turn to suffer, and the men took him and began to crucify him. The whole time these men were beating, whipping, and crucifying Peter, they demanded that he deny that Jesus was the Christ. They said they would take it easy on him if he denied Jesus. Peter would not, and they proceeded to nail him to a wooden cross.

The soldiers were about to drop the cross into the ground when Peter lets out a shout: "Please, please, not like this!" The soldiers thought they had broken him and he would now, at the height of his pain and suffering, deny faith in Jesus. Peter finished his claim, "Please don't crucify me like you did my Savior…. I am not worthy to die like Him. Please crucify me upside down. Jesus is everything, and I am nothing."

I don't know why they agreed to do it, but the soldiers turned Peter's cross upside down and dropped it into the ground. Peter died...and found himself in heaven with the One who died for him.

The audience stands to their feet for a millennium of praise and glory to God. Jesus steps out onto the stage and hugs Simon Peter as Peter exclaims over and over, "Thank You, Jesus, for giving me another chance!"

Jesus begins to speak, and the crowd hushes so quickly the reverberations in the Hall of Heroes resonates in perfect harmony with Christ's next words: "Peter, you made a lot of mistakes, you denied Me three times, you let Me down time and time again...but Peter...*you finished well*. Well done, My good and faithful servant!" I can tell you that I live to hear those words! That one day Jesus would say that to me...I am willing to do anything for that!

The lights go down on the *Rock Talk* show, and the cameras are turned off as people begin to leave. Jesus grabs a camera and a microphone and floats through the crowd asking this question, "You heard what Solomon, David, John, and Peter did for Me. What did you do for Me with the time that I gave you?" What will we be able to say? Will you and I have anything noteworthy to add to this celebration of life? We must be determined that we will live in a manner consistent with our forebears. We must reach people and score for Jesus.

Win People. Make Disciples. Score!

We often try to find a theology about our current life-style that agrees with our misgivings. We invite people to church like that was God's commandment, and we go on mission trips to share our faith in other countries among people whose language we don't even speak, but we neglect those with whom we *can* communicate. God has not called us to be merely church hosts and doormen at the gates of mercy. God wants more from us. *Make disciples.*

Maybe part of the problem lies in the fact that our unbelieving friends and acquaintances don't know us for the follower of Christ that we believe ourselves to be. If we don't open our big mouths and say something to them about Christ, they will never know Him! Maybe we don't want them to know, because it would limit our options. They would not invite us to the parties, golf outings, beach vacations, and visits to the bar. Like the Israelites, our purpose goes up in the toss of a sword and a shield, and we start running from the things of God and running with people who have no inclination toward Him. No, we must run toward victory. It's time to strike and win this fight!

The only way to win this fight is to score, and in order to score we must win people over to a relationship with Jesus Christ. Do you desire to make a difference in your world? Many people talk a good game before their opportunity, but when it is time to act, they get quiet. I have met some strong, muscular, imposing characters, and when I go out to coffee with them, their true mettle is tested. At the coffee shop I will strike up conversations with many people and see if anyone "bites." I find it quite interesting that when someone has been established as a divine appointment for me to share Jesus with them, sharing my faith and being a light to them is simple. Often my strong-looking friend will struggle with what to say and how to say it...I'll then ask, "Have you ever shared your faith with someone?" Invariably they will tell me, "No," or "Very little." How are we supposed to take over the world for Jesus if we don't share Him with the world?

CHAPTER 13

KILL AND TAKE CARE
OF BUSINESS

THIS IS THE MOMENT WHEN WE GET TO REVISIT the purpose of a king, a shepherd, and a soldier in the army of Israel: our purpose is *to kill people and take their stuff*. I still feel like you haven't said it enough, so please say this aloud: "My purpose for the kingdom of God is to kill people and take their stuff for Jesus!" Now, don't you feel better? I do! I am activating your victorious weapon against sin and hell. Your best weapon is communication.

Have you ever watched one of those super-spy movies where the bad guy is standing in front of the good guy with a gun pointed at him and then the bad guy begins a monologue? Have you ever watched his whole diatribe and thought to yourself, "Just shoot him now, and it's over"? I just don't get it. If there was someone out there who was completely focused on destroying my family and me, why would I gain the upper hand and then not finish them off, instead letting them keep talking? (This is all fictional thinking. I really don't wish to harm people, really!) Why sit there conversing with them and saying all kinds of crazy things about how you're going to strap them to a ballistic missile and shoot them into space where their blood will begin to boil and then they will die an agonizing death? OK, I guess you can see that I feel quite passionately about victory. Victory must be taken immediately and without distraction.

Face the Facts and Call Sin Out!

The first battle that must be won is the battle within us. How we win this battle is with communication, but waging this battle effectively requires study. I'm not talking about the *Art of War* or any other tactical manual written. I am talking about the Bible. The battle to defeat sin requires that we follow the mandate of repentance in the Word of God.

> If we say that we have no sin, we deceive ourselves, and the truth is not in us. If we confess our sins, He is faithful and just to forgive us our sins and to cleanse us from all unrighteousness. If we say that we have not sinned, we make Him a liar, and His word is not in us.
> —1 JOHN 1:8–10

The champion is before us and mediocrity is behind us; if we proceed, we will have to deal with this big problem. Let's settle this once and for all. Is God to be victorious in us, or will we allow sin to remain undefeated? The next step is vital to our transformation: face the facts and call it out! When you communicate with God, do not merely *think* your prayers. Don't make God read your mind; faith requires verbal speech.

> ...if you confess with your mouth the Lord Jesus and believe in your heart that God has raised Him from the dead, you will be saved. For with the heart one believes unto righteousness, and with the mouth confession is made unto salvation. For the Scripture says, "Whoever believes on Him will not be put to shame." For there is no distinction between Jew and Greek, for the same Lord over all is rich to all who call upon Him. For "whoever calls on the name of the LORD shall be saved."
> —ROMANS 10:9–13

I'm not trying to be religious and mess with people's traditions and norms for the sake of coming up with *my way*, making people subject to my ideals. You may have been *thinking* prayers that should be *spoken*. God wants you to trust Him with your words. Your words carry weight and influence. What you say is heard in heaven and reverberates in the halls of hell. What would you like the physical world and the spiritual world to hear coming from you? God is not going to ignore your thoughts. He knows your thoughts as well as your actions, but faith is in your actions. Faith is not merely believing, but also putting belief into action. Let's put this battle into action right now:

1. Confess to God everything that you know has been separating you from having the kind of relationship you desire with Him (sins). Take your time and tell Him what you did. Tell Him why you did these things and what you felt during the temptation and completion of this act of sin. Do not hold back on the details. Prayer is communication with God; tell the Lord your complete story. Don't be cheap with your words.

Get a Heart Transplant

The next step is quite valuable to me. There have been times in my life when I would commit sin and I would feel no remorse or sadness about it. I would just go on with life, and it was as if I never made the mistake to begin with. I actually remember times when I actually felt guilty about not feeling guilty. When I asked God for wisdom about this, He shared with me that I had become miscalibrated to His Holy Spirit. The Holy Spirit is the One who convicts the world in regard to sin and righteousness. When we lose our conscience, it is really an indication that we have hardened hearts toward God, and we must break up that hardness with the power of the Holy Spirit.

> Create in me a clean heart, O God, and renew
> a steadfast spirit within me. Do not cast me
> away from Your presence, and do not take
> Your Holy Spirit from me.
>
> —PSALM 51:10–11

David asked God to give him a heart transplant. He wanted a clean and fresh start. The key to his success was his prayer that requested a steadfast spirit within him. This is the part of recalibration that we need! Pray that for you, but let's go a step further. Our feelings are usually not in line with spiritual things when our flesh has been allowed to reign. Let's request this renewal of spirit and a resensitizing of emotion to spiritual things.

2. Recount all the evil sins that you have allowed to permeate your life, and tell the Lord how sorry you are for each one of them. Confess your status of sorrow for sin, even before it manifests in your emotions. Your feelings will follow your faith. You will recognize your sensitivity increasing toward the Lord, and your heart will be renewed.

> Restore to me the joy of Your salvation, and
> uphold me by Your generous Spirit. Then I
> will teach transgressors Your ways, and sin-
> ners shall be converted to You.
>
> —PSALM 51:12–13

3. Ask the Lord to forgive you for all these things, and tell Him what you are feeling,

thinking, and planning for your victory. What are you going to do with your freedom from sin? How are you going to invest God's precious grace?

"I Declare War!"

Now that you've claimed your victory from sin and devilish distractions from within, it's now time to fight the battles around us. *We* have to kill the sin that desires to destroy us. God will help us knock it down, but then it is up to us to kill it and cut its head off! How do we accomplish this task? Open warfare!

The tactics of battle strategies in the Bible are different from many tactics found in other places. I have heard many people quote the scriptures that say the enemy will come and attack, but if we resist him, he will flee seven ways. That scripture is powerfully accurate when it comes to the spiritual battles that we face. However, most of the temptations that we encounter in our lives are centered around the people with whom we associate. These people are generally not going to run screaming seven ways (unless they have a multiple personality disorder), embed themselves in pigs, and rush off a cliff into the sea. For those situations we have to understand proper battle strategies against sin.

There are phrases that go through our minds when it comes to putting ourselves in troublesome and devastating danger: "I can handle it" or "I'm OK" are two of these phrases. We may say these things even when we are walking right into the lions' den. Knowing that we are wearing a garment made of gazelle meat, we shouldn't be there. But for some strange reason we present ourselves to problematic postures in the midst of familiar sin. We have to run from these things. Running will not make us look cool or "victorious." But is success appearance or is it action? There were times when I had to hide from friends who would always invite me out to do things to which I knew I couldn't say no. I would rather hide and pretend I wasn't in my dorm room than fail and sin against the Lord. This temptation to dance on the edge of a knife is an attitude of destruction. It's a choice that must be denounced and avoided. By our very spiritual nature you and I cannot "handle" sinful situations and temptations. That is pride at its harmful best, and it is the beginning of a major failure in our lives.

> Therefore if anyone cleanses himself from the latter, he will be a vessel for honor, sanctified and useful for the Master, prepared for every good work. Flee also youthful lusts; but pursue righteousness, faith, love, and peace with those who call on the Lord out of a pure heart. But avoid foolish and ignorant disputes, knowing that they generate strife.
>
> —2 TIMOTHY 2:21–23

When we're living our lives out of focus with our purpose, we get into arguments about what we think sin is or isn't. When we are in tune with our divine purpose and place in God's kingdom, we spend our time trying to reach people with the love of Jesus. Our breath is spent doing productive things that have eternal significance. When we fight battles for the souls of those around us, we treat their lives as precious and delicate. We are not the ogres of Christ; we are the under-shepherds of the "Good Shepherd."

The Victory Is in Your Mouth

Sometimes I talk too much! I get excited about things that are to come and situations that are intellectually stimulating, and I'll talk all the way through them. If you don't like overtalkers, you'd be in big trouble with me. I am one of those people whom you probably loathe, because I talk in the movie theater or to my television during a riveting movie or program! I figure that if I paid the big money for the ticket and even more money for popcorn and other concessions, I deserve to add my commentary to the soundtrack. My comments can range from the banal to the ridiculous: "Why are they doing that? Don't go in there! I told you! Run, girl! Eat all that food! Run! What are you doing? Run, fool, run!" I have good news for all my fellow outspoken believers: victory in the battle for souls requires you to talk! My pastor would say, "Your victory is right underneath your nose; it's in your mouth!" All we have to do is open our big mouths, and people will be transformed forever.

Don't be surprised when people talk back. When we are endeavoring to share what God has for people, they won't all sit quietly and listen. Some may even become

quite hostile and desire to engage in an intellectual argument. Remember that your purpose requires humility
and kindness in order to achieve victory.

When David headed down into the Valley of Elah to
face off with the champion Goliath from Gath, Goliath
saw David and became even more upset because he
thought King Saul was trying to prank him by sending
this young, inexperienced boy to face off with him in
battle. He had neither seen David before, nor had he
heard songs about his prowess in battle.

> So the Philistine came, and began drawing
> near to David, and the man who bore the shield
> went before him. And when the Philistine
> looked about and saw David, he disdained
> him; for he was only a youth, ruddy and good-
> looking. So the Philistine said to David, "Am I
> a dog, that you come to me with sticks?" And
> the Philistine cursed David by his gods. And
> the Philistine said to David, "Come to me, and
> I will give your flesh to the birds of the air and
> the beasts of the field!"
> —1 SAMUEL 17:41–44

Can you imagine a shepherd walking out onto a
battlefield with only a staff and a slingshot? The enemy
soldier had all the battle garb and weapons one could
be equipped with, plus an armor bearer with a shield.
Goliath saw a young man with no armor, no shield, and
no sword...how could this boy possibly win against this
mighty nine-foot-tall warrior? He would win because

Goliath was a dog! The Scriptures describe dogs as vile things in the community, animals that would eat whatever was presented to them without the righteous discrimination of a servant of Christ. Revelation also describes these persons as those who do things under the power of their own human means and strength, denying the power of God to incite a change with or without. Goliath was one man whose physical prowess had helped him accomplish much. He thought his own human power would equip him to destroy God's son, David.

But David didn't come to this fight in his own strength. Had David come to defeat Goliath in human strength, he would have probably brought a bow and a bunch of arrows. He would then have shot arrows at Goliath from a long distance and never advanced near this huge beast of a man. That's what I would have done. I don't like getting beat up, and being beaten to death...no, that would not be fun!

On the contrary, David responded to Goliath with the words of a man of faith, knowing it was the Lord who would help him:

> Then David said to the Philistine, "You come to me with a sword, with a spear, and with a javelin. But I come to you in the name of the LORD of hosts, the God of the armies of Israel, whom you have defied. This day the LORD will deliver you into my hand, and I will strike you and take your head from you. And this day I will give the carcasses of the camp of the Philistines to the birds of the air and the

wild beasts of the earth, that all the earth may
know that there is a God in Israel. Then all this
assembly shall know that the LORD does not
save with sword and spear; for the battle is the
LORD's, and He will give you into our hands."

—1 SAMUEL 17:45–47

David not only declared victory over the champion Goliath, but he also made the assertion that Israel
would claim victory over all the army of the Philistines!
That was bold talk for a shepherd boy. What can I say?
Confidence is sexy! If we are going to impact lives, we
have to put our confidence in Christ and speak boldly
about Him. Faith is not mere bragging, but you cannot
brag when you talk about what God can do…because
He is able to do the impossible. Be bold! Speak with
kindness, but challenge convention.

The Kingdom of God Is Not
Just Talk; It's Power!

I often meet people who tell me they are either athe-
ists or agnostics. I love the challenge of sharing my faith
with them. In the past I would get caught up in theo-
logical discussions, trying to convince them that I was
on the right track in my faith. I've learned since that discussion alone is not enough. I began to get bolder in my
approach and began to challenge them and promote the
power of God to them. The kingdom of God is not just
that of talk, but it's power.

I asked one man, since he thought there was no God, if I could pray with him. I told him that he would feel the presence of God when we prayed. I prayed a simple prayer with passion on that airplane, and this man began to cry and shake. He said, "I felt God! What did you do? I felt something! What is this? What did you do?" I told him that God is real. After we prayed for his salvation, I said, "Now, I dare you to go to a Bible-believing church in your hometown and experience all that God has in store for you! It's going to be awesome!"

People want someone with passion for what is truly real to reach out to them and share faith, hope, and love. I have reached more people talking about the love of God and the peace that He brings than anything else.

An admitted atheist accepted Jesus in the O'Hare International Airport when I prayed for his sister-in-law and the Lord healed her knee on the spot. God, in His infinite wisdom, put His gospel in the hands of weak and feeble men and women. We are not to be strong for ourselves, but strong in the Lord and in His mighty power! Don't be afraid to fail; be afraid to quit! If you fail, it is normal for man, but if you quit, you miss out on the glory of battle! How can we go from "glory (glorious victory) to glory (glorious victory)" if there's no battle? Fortune favors the bold.

You Must Cut Off the Enemy's Head

David reminded Goliath that he was not battling a shepherd boy with a rock and a sling with a staff for backup, but Goliath was fighting against the God of Israel. God had promised Israel the land and the subjection of its inhabitants in the Promised Land. It was time for them to possess that land, and if it took a young, inexperienced warrior to accomplish that, so be it!

After David's bold claims, Goliath grew furious and came toward him in a rage. David was still not afraid.

> So it was, when the Philistine arose and came and drew near to meet David, that *David hurried and ran toward the army to meet the Philistine.* Then David put his hand in his bag and took out a stone; and he slung it and struck the Philistine in his forehead, so that the stone sank into his forehead, and he fell on his face to the earth. So David prevailed over the Philistine with a sling and a stone, and struck the Philistine and killed him. But there was no sword in the hand of David. Therefore David ran and stood over the Philistine, took his sword and drew it out of its sheath and killed him, and cut off his head with it.
>
> —1 SAMUEL 17:48–51,
> EMPHASIS ADDED

David didn't wait for this huge champion to come to him. *David ran* and crossed the battle line to meet Goliath! Can you imagine what must have gone through this huge warrior's mind? This little pipsqueak had just insulted him and told him that he was going to kill him and cut off his head.

As the champion rose to go fight David, the shepherd didn't shrink back or even gulp in fear; he jumped to attention and started running...*running*...toward Goliath! That is awesome! David grabbed the stone, swung the sling, and in an *alley-oop* to God, struck Goliath in his forehead. (Many historians believe he hit Goliath in the eye.) This was more than a lucky shot; it was a God-given knockout blow. The champion's helmet had to cover his head, and the only accessible area would have been his eyes and cheeks. What a shot! Goliath fell facedown, and David finished what he started. Taking Goliath's own sword, he killed the champion and cut off his head. When he lifted the head into the air in victory, the Philistine army's hearts sank. Israel was victorious, and Philistia fell to them that day.

This powerful story takes an unexpected turn right after the battle ends. It seems that David had a penchant for booty. But what special treasure did he extract? Gold, silver, or precious stones from the treasury of the Philistines?

> And David took the head of the Philistine and
> brought it to Jerusalem, but he put his armor
> in his tent.
> —1 SAMUEL 17:54

Wait...this is kind of gross! Why did David take Goliath's head with him? Of course, everyone would believe that he won, since the entire Israeli army had just watched him slaughter the Philistine champion. Why take his head? David was doing several things in this scene that are important. First, David proved that Goliath was dead; he would not recover from his battle wounds and then rise again to fight another day. David took Goliath's identity; the body would have no face and therefore was desecrated in the traditions of burial. Finally, David provided inspiration; the people of Israel would very soon face more insurmountable odds, and this head would remind them that what seems impossible to man is possible with God. I still think it's gross, but it's also kind of cool.

David not only took Goliath's head; he took Goliath's armor. The armor was not taken to Jerusalem and presented to Saul. The armor was placed in David's tent, with David's things. What was the significance of taking the champion's armor? Goliath wasn't the only big warrior who lived in Gath; there were many more. In fact, Goliath had four brothers who are described in Scripture, and one of them was supposed to have been mightier than Goliath and the others. The Scriptures describe four brothers who were "born to the giant in Gath" (Goliath's father; 2 Sam. 21:22): Ishbibenob—whom Abishai later killed, Sath, Lahmi, and an unnamed man with six fingers and six toes. Any one of these warriors could have easily come back to the valley the next week and opposed Israel again. Could you imagine Ishbi-Benob dressed up in Goliath's armor, shouting the daily insults to Israel? The people would have lost heart and panicked again, thinking that Goliath had raised himself up and come back to fight them again! Not possible when David had his head. However, the armor could have been redressed, and the intimidation and death would begin again. David withdrew any opportunity for the enemy of Israel to attack again the same way. David removed the armor of the enemy from the field of battle. Goliath's sword, shield, spear, javelin, and armor would never again be used against David or the armies of Israel.

When you defeat your champion, you have a responsibility to your fellow brothers and sisters. The battle is not over when you knock sin down. You must cut the head off of this life-controlling sin and show it to the world. You must tell those around you how the enemy tried to attack you and then share what you did to overcome the sinful advance. When you tell people what God has helped you do to live this victorious life you enjoy, you are removing the weapons of the enemy from the field of battle in their lives.

There's Strength in Numbers

One of the enemy's most effective tactics against the people of God is to divide and conquer. Have you ever felt as if you were the only one who seemed to be dealing with the problems that you faced? Like there couldn't be another person on earth who could possibly understand the amount of pressure and problems that you have to endure? You have brothers and sisters who feel as if they are alone, as well. They may not be able to understand what you are facing, but you can understand them. Our lives cannot be victorious if they are isolated from others. The victory that we seek and the victory that others are seeking are intrinsically linked. We must share what God has equipped us with to overcome. This will inspire people to overcome the trials of their lives.

The enemy has many people backed into a corner. They want to be free, they need to be free, they were born to be free of sin, but without you they are doomed to face the same repetitive lifestyle of mediocrity that got them into their mess in the first place. They need examples of people who have overcome the things with which they struggle: gossip, abuse, lying, divorce, pornography, unforgiveness, greed, filthy speech, anger, lust, hurt, and addiction. We cannot simply show them a life that seems like a dream and then tell them, "Sorry that *you* struggle with that sin thing. I'm just naturally a better person than you! Good luck!"

No, we have to tell them what we overcame and let them know that it is possible to live victoriously and defeat the undefeated things in our lives. How do we do this? The anointing! The anointing is not the power of God to be better than others. The anointing is the power of God to live holy and tell people about the life that we are living with the convincing of the Holy Spirit to back up our words. When we don't know what to say or how to speak to people about our victory, the Holy Spirit will speak through us to share our Lord's heart.

When we keep our experiences to ourselves and refuse to share the "embarrassing" antics of our past failures, we are placing weapons into the hands of our enemy to be used effectively in the lives of others. We become the champion's armor bearer. We march around in our own victory and stand by while the champion of undefeated sin pummels, chops, and beats our brothers and sisters to death. We have to cross the line and switch sides. The armor bearer for a soldier is learning the ropes of war so that he can himself become effective in battle one day. This is not how we are to proceed. We are not supposed to let other people "pay their dues" and struggle while we maintain the answers to their problems, weapons that are sharpened and well oiled, locked up within ourselves. We must remove the champion's weapons, so that he has nothing from us to equip against those he despises.

The enemy has been taking the heads of our brothers and sisters instead of the other way around. He keeps diluting their understanding of their identity by affixing who they are to their sins and wrongdoings. They believe that they are recovering alcoholics, former drug addicts, or divorcees. But that's not how God sees them. God has called us to be more than our past, but they won't know how if we don't tell them how we did it ourselves:

> But you are a chosen generation, a royal priesthood, a holy nation, His own special people, that you may proclaim the praises of Him who called you out of darkness into His marvelous light; who once were not a people but are now the people of God, who had not obtained mercy but now have obtained mercy.
>
> —1 PETER 2:9–10

David taught his mighty men, and it was these men of honor and power who dispatched the remaining brothers of Goliath of Gath. If David hadn't invested the things that he knew in those whom he led, he himself would have fallen to the family of Goliath.

> Moreover the Philistines had yet war again with Israel; and David went down, and his servants with him, and fought against the Philistines: and David waxed faint. And Ishbibenob, which was of the sons of the giant, the weight of whose spear weighed three hundred shekels of brass in weight, he being girded with a new sword, thought to have slain David. But Abishai the son of Zeruiah succoured him, and smote the Philistine, and killed him. Then the men of David sware unto him, saying, Thou shalt go no more out with us to battle, that thou quench not the light of Israel.
>
> —2 SAMUEL 21:15–17, KJV

When we remove the weapons of our enemy from the field of battle for our brothers and sisters, they too become mighty for the Lord. Our fellow warriors will then be there for us when we face champions that we aren't equipped to fight. We can lean on them, and their wisdom will help us fight our continuous battle for victorious living.

CHAPTER 14

MODERN PLUNDER

READ IN YOUR BEST PIRATE ACCENT: *ARRRGH! Ahoy! Let's attack these limey slugs and take their gooooold! They thinks they can come here and tote these treasures through our waters. Ha! We'll show them all!*

I love a good pirate story. There's something special about a swashbuckling tale of the antics of a captain and his crew seizing treasure and adventure from the foamy surf. I often imagine myself as a mighty pirate, and the lives of lost people are my treasure! I sail into their lives, and they are never the same! Sometimes I get to swing through unannounced in seemingly random occurrences, but they're not random to my captain. Jesus, the pirate of peace, set them all up. Our treasure is the same as His treasure. Our goals are the same as His. We are not going after gold, silver, or costly stones. The treasure and currency of heaven are not those things. The

Bible clearly describes the streets of heaven as paved with gold. Gold cannot mean too much to them there when they pave the roads with it. (Hey, God, when You do a remodel up there, could You throw some road tar down on Your son here?) Silver and precious stones are described in John the Revelator's accounts of oceans and buildings and structures in heaven. Again, we don't build homes and structures with our most precious items. I've never seen someone bottling up ocean water as the greatest treasure on earth. These things cannot be the most precious valuables to the Lord.

The Currency of Heaven

The most valued thing on earth is money, or currency. People will do anything to get it. So many people work themselves to death for the prospect of getting more of it. The potential achievement of currency has caused many to surrender their values and fall into failure. The Bible even states that the love of money is the root of all kinds of evil. No, money matters little to the kingdom of heaven.

The currency of heaven is the thing most celebrated in heaven. It is what all of heaven rejoices over and sings songs about. What causes the angels and the saints to rejoice with great joy while the Father beams with preternatural passion? Souls!

> Or suppose a woman has ten silver coins and
> loses one. Does she not light a lamp, sweep
> the house and search carefully until she finds

it? And when she finds it, she calls her friends and neighbors together and says, "Rejoice with me; I have found my lost coin." In the same way, I tell you, there is rejoicing in the presence of the angels of God over one sinner who repents.

—LUKE 15:8–10, NIV

The currency of heaven is not the silver coin; it's people! Heaven is loud with rejoicing and singing all the time. Every few seconds someone accepts Jesus Christ as their Lord and Savior! Have you been putting souls in heaven's bank? Have you caused the Lord to dance and the angels to do flying backflips? Let's go get His treasure! Our Lord requires His sailors to be busy in the work of the kingdom. The question is, will you reject the gold for what's truly important?

Jesus Is With You Through the Fire

Have you ever read the story of Shadrach, Meshach, and Abednego? This shocking story in Daniel 3 shares their battle to obey the laws of the Lord rather than the decrees of King Nebuchadnezzar. When they decided not to worship before the golden idol that Nebuchadnezzar erected, the king gave them another chance to comply with his decree and bow down. They told the king they would rather die than obey his command and dishonor God. Nebuchadnezzar raged against these men and commanded that his men heat up the furnace seven times hotter than usual. (Does he burn people to death all the time?) The king then commanded his men to throw Shadrach, Meshach, and Abednego into the fiery furnace. But instead of these three Hebrew men being killed, the king was shocked to see four men in the fire, unharmed, and the fourth he described as the "Son of God" (v. 25). When he called these heroes out of the flames, he was amazed to see "...men on whose bodies the fire had no power" (v. 27). Their hair wasn't burned, their clothes weren't burned, and they didn't even smell like smoke!

With all that your enemy has tried to do, it's sometimes hard to believe that the Lord is going to turn it all around. It may seem like you are heading down and there's nothing that can stop it. I want to remind you that you serve the God of the impossible. Jesus told the disciples, "With God all things are possible" (Matt. 19:26). Jesus was not visible to Shadrach, Meshach, and Abednego before the furnace or after the furnace. He was seen only *in* the furnace!

> God is our refuge and strength, a very present
> help in trouble. Therefore we will not fear, even
> though the earth be removed, and though the
> mountains be carried into the midst of the
> sea; though its waters roar and be troubled,
> though the mountains shake with its swelling.
> —PSALM 46:1–3

This psalmist understood how Jesus is positioned in relation to all the battles that we must fight to attain and maintain our victorious life. Our Jesus is a very present help...when? *In* the time of trouble! Jesus is *in your trouble*! In fact, when all your friends and acquaintances run, Jesus will come to your aid. He is not afraid of the problems and issues that you and I face. Jesus is the Alpha and the Omega (Rev. 1:8, 11; 21:16; 22:13). I imagine that Jesus is able to be everywhere at once, and He is not limited to time or space. He exists above the laws of earth and nature. If you are wondering where Jesus might be in your situation, think of the Hebrew boys in that fiery furnace and remember, Jesus is in this with you. Jesus is ahead of you, in the midst of the biggest problem you will ever face. He's cheering you on in the midst of this huge battle and saying to you today, "C'mon! You can do this! I am with you! It's rough up here at this point of your life, you're going to endure some things, but I am here, and I will walk you through this! If you can't walk anymore, I will carry you! I love you! Let's go!" I'm telling you, this victory is not something you should be content for on your own. All of heaven is cheering you on, and Jesus declares He will be with you. You can do this!

"You Don't Smell Like Smoke"

The part of Shadrach, Meshach, and Abednego's story that I enjoy the most (other than saying their names and hearing other people mess them up too) is the conclusion. I love the fact that when they came out of the fire, there was no physical indication that they *had ever even been thrown into the fire!* The Word says that they didn't even smell like smoke (Dan. 3:27)! That is awesome, and that is what's happening to you today. You may not have been focusing on it, but you've been through some fires yourself. You have faced your champion and have done battle with the things in your life that want to destroy your faith. You have arisen victorious because the famous One has brought you through with His grace and mercy. Now there's a great and tremendous problem that you have to face. You don't smell like smoke. That's right. People whom you will meet tomorrow, and the next day, and so forth...they can't tell you ever dealt with the sins and struggles that you have defeated. They may walk by you and sniff you and they will smell the anointing of Jesus, nothing else! While you and I may celebrate that fact in our hearts, that itself is also the problem. People need to hear from you about what the Lord has brought you through. If you keep these stories to yourself, you have missed the point of going through them in the first place. God wants us to tell people what He is able to do when we put our trust in Him.

After such victories, you are also going to inherit a tribe of people around you called "haters." These are people that wake up at "hate-o'clock" in the morning and drink "Haterade." They will be the first ones to talk to you about your transformation, and they will try to belittle your history. They will try to tell you that you didn't really endure that much or there would have been much more "collateral damage" in your life. They assume that suffering is the lifestyle of the spiritually sensitive, and therefore their lack of overcoming is due to their sincere walk with God. These people will say, "Look at that David! There's no way he used to struggle with that addiction; he's probably just saying that. His life looks perfect: job, wife, kids, great home, and he can even sing! He's got it all; he doesn't even smell of smoke!" Or, "I thought she said that she endured all kinds of abuse growing up. Why then does she so freely love these kids in the children's church? She was probably exaggerating, because people don't just overcome situations like hers. I bet it never happened; she doesn't even smell like smoke!"

Your Testimony Has Power

While it is not our job to make the haters more uncomfortable, we must speak the truth about what God has done for us. Tell them! Even if they don't believe or won't receive, tell them. (OK, that reminds me of an old Andraé Crouch song, but it's still good!)

We cannot hide in the blessings and promises and not share the process. That only leads people into disillusionment and despair. Your testimony has power.

And I heard a loud voice saying in heaven, Now is come salvation, and strength, and the kingdom of our God, and the power of his Christ: for the accuser of our brethren is cast down, which accused them before our God day and night. And they overcame him by the blood of the Lamb, *and by the word of their*

testimony; and they loved not their lives unto
the death.
—REVELATION 12:10–11, KJV,
EMPHASIS ADDED

When you tell others what the Lord has done for you, you are building their faith, your faith, and praising the One who blessed your life. It's a win-win-win! The testimonies that many people have shared with me over the years have shaped my life and calling. I keep a file folder with printouts of people's testimonies, and it encourages me when I reread them. Reading them reminds me that I am on the right track. It reminds me that everyone is facing a champion of some sort. It reminds me to take time to hear their hearts and help point them toward the victorious warrior.

After a week of speaking in motivational public school assemblies, I was approached by a young lady named Kara by the stage. She was all blacked out: black lipstick, makeup, clothes, and hair. She had a small spider tattoo on her neck. I haven't seen too many fifteen-year-olds with tattoos, and it caught my eye as she said, "Thanks for coming here. It seems like you really do love us." The local pastors and I got a moment to talk with her during the school's second period lunch and invite her to our evangelistic portion of the weeks' events. She came! I'll never forget the rock band we had for our evangelistic rally. They were as excellent as they were crazy! Jumping around, running, crowd surfing! It was a sight to behold, and Kara seemed to love it! As I gave the invitation for people to accept Jesus Christ, she was one of the first people to come forward and pray with us. At the end of the evening she stopped by our booth and asked for a business card. Then Kara said something strange, "I think you changed my life…but I'll write you tomorrow and let you know for sure." I didn't know what else to say but "OK," and then she walked back over to her friends, crying and hugging them with joy.

The following morning I was in my connection city of Denver when my ministry mobile phone started getting messages. It was Kara! She was the fastest phone keyboard typist in the universe. I cannot believe how many words she sent in just minutes, but every sentence of her correspondence was incredible to me. Her story was a sad one.

Kara was born to a mother who did not want her. Her biological mother had been raped and wanted to abort the baby. Her grandmother told her mother that if she would go through with the pregnancy, she would care for the child. This kind grandmother saved Kara's life. Her mother was even heard by family members screaming how she didn't want the baby while giving birth. After her hospital recovery, she didn't see the infant Kara again for months. Kara was even named by her grandmother. Kara never got to spend time with her biological mother while growing up. Since she lived with her grandmother, her biological mom would periodically stop by to visit. Every time Kara would try to come around to see her mom, her mom would reject her. It was either too early to hang out or too late, and she was told to go to bed. Many times she hid behind a wall in the house just to listen to her mom talking to grandmother. She remembered thinking, "I wish she would talk to me like that." She would cough and try to make a little noise so that they knew she was there, thinking maybe, just maybe they would invite her to come over to the table and let her spend time with her real mom, just once. But every time they discovered little Kara, her mom would say, "Go to bed. I'll see you in the morning!" And by the next morning her mom would be long gone.

Finally Kara had a breakthrough. She woke up one Saturday morning and her mother was still at the house! She was passed out on the couch in the living room. Kara was so overjoyed she didn't know what to do. She went over all the things she wanted to do with her mommy that day, and with a big smile she walked toward her sleeping prodigal parent. Kara slid up next to her mom, and before she said a word, she touched her mom's hair and compared it to her own. "I've got Mommy's hair." She leaned over and sniffed her mother, and she said it was one of her greatest moments as she thought, "That's what a mommy smells like." (She smelled her mother for the first time at eleven years old.)

Kara touched her mother's shoulder and said, "Mommy! You're still here! Can we play now? Let's play, Mommy! Can we—"

All of a sudden Kara's mom jumped up and screamed at the child in a drunken rage, "Get away from me! Get away from me! I don't want to see you! You remind me of everything that ever went wrong in my life! I hate you! I don't want to see you!"

Kara ran back to her room crying. She couldn't understand why her mother didn't want to spend any time with her. She thought she'd been a bad girl and maybe her mom knew that she sometimes lied and stole things. She never again tried to see her mom, and her mom's visits became even scarcer.

When we arrived at her high school to promote positive life choices, Kara had not seen her mom in over three years. She said she felt alone, like no one cared. At the end of my assembly program I tell the students that I love them and I care. Kara said that I was the first stranger who had ever said that to her, and she felt like it was true. She came to the evangelistic rally just wanting to feel that love in her heart again. When we gave the invitation to receive Christ, she said to herself, "I'll give this a try...but I'll know if this Jesus guy really loves me if He's still there in the morning." That is why she said, "I think what you said changed my life, but I'll let you know in the morning."

As Kara typed the rest of her long discourse, I began to audibly weep in the airport, and the people standing around me got scared. (When a six-foot-three-inch-tall, athletic-looking man begins to cry aloud, people get nervous.) She wrote: "Guess what, Mr. Allen? I felt Jesus in my heart last night...I didn't want to go to sleep because it felt so good to feel love and not be alone. I was scared that He was only with me for the night and that I would be alone again in the morning. But guess what? He's still here! I can feel His love, and I know He won't leave me now! He's still here!" Since I met young Kara, there have been hundreds of thousands of air miles traveled. I have ministered and motivated on five of seven continents. I have traveled around the world many times, but I am not tired. Kara has given me enough fuel for a lifetime.

Our testimony has power. How do I know? Look at the warring shepherd, David. He was allowed to march right into a battle with the most prolific champion that the Philistines would employ. David would fight to the death with an undefeated foe that stood nearly ten feet tall. The weapons that Goliath possessed were frightening without ever being used. The presence of this foe was so alarming, the Israeli army stood at attention for forty days and nights and no one even tried to fight him. By the time David got to the battle lines, the men were fleeing at the very sight of Goliath, and he hadn't killed or even hurt anyone. Why would King Saul allow this virtually inexperienced shepherd to fight a one-on-one battle for the fate of the nation of Israel? Why would the king risk his entire kingdom and allow David to represent the whole of that nation? Why would the king put the future of his children and his children's children into the hands of a slingshot-carrying, staff-waving sheepherder?

Because David had a testimony!

> And Saul said to David, "You are not able to
> go against this Philistine to fight with him; for
> you are a youth, and he a man of war from

his youth." But David said to Saul, "Your servant used to keep his father's sheep, and when
a lion or a bear came and took a lamb out of
the flock, I went out after it and struck it, and
delivered the lamb from its mouth; and when
it arose against me, I caught it by its beard,
and struck and killed it. Your servant has
killed both lion and bear; and this uncircumcised Philistine will be like one of them, seeing
he has defied the armies of the living God."
Moreover David said, "The LORD, who delivered me from the paw of the lion and from
the paw of the bear, He will deliver me from
the hand of this Philistine." And Saul said to
David, "Go, and the LORD be with you!"

—1 SAMUEL 17:33–37

The first time I read this account of David's experiences as a shepherd, I thought to myself, "This caring-
for-sheep thing is a lot more exciting than I thought!"
David has an incredible story here! After hearing a testimony like that, I would be just like King Saul: "You go,
boy! Go get 'em!"

You see, our greatest tool in overcoming the enemy
is our testimony. The greatest weapon we have to overcome the undefeated champion is the stories from our
lives and others where Jesus earlier won our hearts
and souls from the jaws of defeat and death. When we
remember and relive those events, it gives us courage to
go on fighting new and bigger and "badder" foes.

I cannot forget the testimony night my church used to have when I was growing up. So many times people would share their experiences and some of the harrowing things they endured, to then give God the praise for saving the day. I used to love those Sunday nights at church. We would sing songs about the cross and the blood that Jesus shed in payment for our redemption. It was a time of warmth and caring. We would hear about church members' greatest failures and some of their worst decisions. We heard about addictions, infidelity, physical and sexual abuse, and problems that made many others feel as if they had lived in a fairy tale most of their lives. These stories began as dark as the sins they contained. But there was one thread of light that connected all of them. They all contained the intervention of the Savior and promoted the life that was later enjoyed by the testifier.

Many people today do not understand what a testimony is and does! I have heard people tell stories from their lives in an apparent attempt at "shock and awe," trying to elicit a response from the listener. *It's not wise* to share our testimony *in an effort* to amaze people or to gain their sympathies. We are to share our story of transformation so that others are encouraged and built up in the message of hope! The proper ratio of test versus triumph should be such that people have a general understanding of your problems, hear a full account of God's effect in your life, and learn about the journey that now prevails over the problem. Who is the champion now? We win as we share *the solution* and *the success* that the Lord has brought us. Whenever we concentrate too much on the "juicy sin" bits, people get disillusioned into thinking that they can fail and then lean on a gravy train of grace to save the day. Our testimony must promote the victory, not the greatness of our former depravity.

David told the king of the greatness of God's mercy, love, and power! He told the king that he had killed the lion (the champion of the jungle) and the bear (the champion of the forest) with his shepherding gear and his bare hands...and he would defeat this champion over Israel as if he were one of them. And he was right!

> And when the Philistines saw that their champion was dead, they fled. Now the men of Israel and Judah arose and shouted, and pursued the Philistines as far as the entrance of the valley and to the gates of Ekron. And the wounded of the Philistines fell along the road to Shaaraim, even as far as Gath and Ekron. Then the children of Israel returned from chasing the Philistines, and they plundered their tents.
>
> —1 SAMUEL 17:51–53

All it took was one man to rise from the remnant and begin an assault on the champion. As soon as the men of Israel saw what could be, they began to fight and defeat champions in their own lives. They chased the enemy all the way down to the gates of the Philistine cities. "We've got the enemy on the run right now! Hell is losing because we are not stopping at the gates...we are going in and taking back the lives of our lost friends, neighbors, and family members!"

> He said to them, "But who do you say that I am?" Simon Peter answered and said, "You are the Christ, the Son of the living God." Jesus answered and said to him, "Blessed are you, Simon Bar-Jonah, for flesh and blood has not revealed this to you, but My Father who is in heaven. And I also say to you that you are Peter, and on this rock I will build My church, and the gates of Hades shall not prevail against it. And I will give you the keys of the kingdom of heaven, and whatever you bind on earth will be bound in heaven, and whatever you loose on earth will be loosed in heaven."
>
> —MATTHEW 16:15–19

Kill the Enemy and Take His Stuff

Let's get something started. Let's start a battle right here, right now. Let's pick a fight with hell. I double dare you to step out of your normal routine and reach the hearts of people with your story. The spoils of this war are great! Did you notice that when the Israelites finished pursuing the enemy, they returned to plunder? Yes! That's your purpose: *kill the enemy (sin) and take his stuff (souls) for the kingdom of God!* The moment you begin to do this, others will follow and the world will never be the same. We will turn the world upside down with our preaching! The king recognized the authority, power, and intensity of one who had a story. Saul sent David to win, and yet he had no idea who he even was!

> When Saul saw David going out against the Philistine, he said to Abner, the commander of the army, "Abner, whose son is this youth?" and Abner said, "As your soul lives, O king, I do not know." So the king said, "Inquire whose son this young man is."
>
> Then, as David returned from the slaughter of the Philistine, Abner took him and brought him before Saul with the head of the Philistine in his hand. And Saul said to him, "Whose son are you, young man?" so David answered, "I am the son of your servant Jesse the Bethle-hemite."
>
> —1 SAMUEL 17:55–58

You are the unnamed generation of greatness. You are the one whom God has chosen to lead this battle and destroy sin from the face of your existence. The enemy has had his way for far too long. It is time for one such as you to rise up and do what needs to be done. Generations before you stood on the sidelines and discussed problems the world over. They cursed the darkness and made little difference. It is time for you to light the candle, dispel the darkness, and draw this generation to the light of God's love. The moment you and I begin to live and fight according to our purpose as victors, the church will awaken.

People are going to approach you at work, at the mall, in online gaming forums, at school, in grocery stores, on Facebook, in the coffee shop, and at church, and they will ask you: "What is it about you that's so different? What are you doing? What are you into?" You will say, "I am the servant of God and a follower of Jesus Christ!" Fireworks will go off, a rock band will start playing "We Are the Champions," men and women will weep for joy, cats and dogs will live together in peace, hot buttered popcorn will fall like rain from the sky, children will obey their parents, french fries will grow up from the ground instead of grass, and oceans will fill with milkshake goodness…Actually, none of that stuff will really happen. However, we *will* tell them how Jesus changed our lives and how He can do the same for them. When we stop and pray the prayer of life-commitment to Christ with them, heaven will tune up its orchestra, Jesus will warm up for another dance, and the angels will ready their wings and voices…what once was undefeated will go to the grave. Heaven will celebrate victory for another precious soul, because you opened your mouth and the champion fell.

NOTES

Chapter 1
Your Valley of Elah

1. Shaquille O'Neal, *Shaq Talks Back* (New York: St. Martin's Press, 2001).

Chapter 2
Fragmented Realities

1. Merriam-Webster.com, s.v. "double-minded," http://www.merriam-webster.com/dictionary/double-minded (accessed February 12, 2013).

Chapter 4
Call It What It Is!

1. *Merriam-Webster's Collegiate Dictionary*, 11th edition (Springfield, MA: Merriam-Webster, Inc., 2003), s.v. "denial."

Part 2
Solution: The Anointing

1. Kenneth Copeland Ministries, "Real Help," http://www.kcm.org/index.php?p=real_help_content&id=1363 (accessed January 9, 2013).

Chapter 5
What Is It? Supernatural!

1. *Merriam-Webster's Collegiate Dictionary*, 11th edition (Springfield, MA: Merriam-Webster, Inc., 2003), s.v. "anoint."
2. Fr. William Saunders, "Straight Answers: Who Were the Magi?", Catholicherald.com, http://catholicherald.com/stories/Straight-Answers-Who-Were-the-Magi,6976 (accessed February 12, 2013).

3. *Merriam-Webster's Collegiate Dictionary*, s.v. "passion."

4. Author heard this statement at the National Youth Workers Conference in Kansas City, Missouri, 2008.

5. Fuchsia Pickett, *Walking in the Anointing of the Holy Spirit* (Lake Mary, FL: Charisma House, 2004), 33.

6. *Sunday Morning*, "Olive Oil: Mining a Liquid Gold," CBS, November 20, 2011, http://www.cbsnews.com/8301 -3445_162-57328308/olive-oil-mining-a-liquid-gold/ (accessed January 9, 2013).

Chapter 7
What Did Jesus Wear?

1. W. E. Vine, s.v. "displeased," *Vine's Expository Dictionary of New Testament Words*, Blue Letter Bible, http:// www.blueletterbible.org/Search/Dictionary/viewTopic.cfm?type =getTopic&Topic=Displeased&DictID=9#Vines (accessed February 12, 2013).

Chapter 8
Oil Change—How to Get It

1. *Merriam-Webster's Collegiate Dictionary*, 11th edition (Springfield, MA: Merriam-Webster, Inc., 2003), s.v. "unity."